T0372522

Talent Management in Latin America

In a period of about 20 years, Latin America (LATAM) moved from having highly unstable closed economies ruled by authoritarian regimes, to becoming more democratic, stable, and open to investment and trade, attracting by 2020 close to 11% of world total foreign direct investment. In parallel, the region has seen the emergence of large multinational companies (so called multilatinas), which have become true global players.

There is still relatively little knowledge about how to manage employees in these countries, and there is a need for more research addressing people management problems. In comparison with other world regions, Human Resource Management (HRM) research on Latin America remains scarce. Focusing on this region, this book seeks to offer a more up to date review of the main developments in HRM and talent management that have recently occurred in Latin America, paying attention to local cultural and institutional factors; illustrate examples of idiosyncratic problems or issues that require approaches to TM that differ significantly from those commonly established in current literature; and describe and reflect on the transfer of talent management policies from and to LATAM within the context of local and foreign multinational companies.

Talent Management in Latin America updates main HRM topics in Latin America, with a local focus on culture and institutions. It shows the latest state of knowledge on the topic and will be of interest both to researchers, academics, and students in the fields of human resource management, critical management studies, and international business.

Jordi Trullen is Associate Professor in the Department of People Management and Organisation at Ramon Llull University, ESADE, Spain.

Jaime Bonache is Professor of Management in the Department of Business Administration at Carlos III University of Madrid, Spain.

Routledge Focus on Issues in Global Talent Management
Series Editor: Ibraiz Tarique
Pace University, USA

Talent Management in Small and Medium Enterprises
Context, Practices and Outcomes
Aleksy Poctowski, Urban Pauli and Alicja Miś

Talent Management in Latin America
Pressing Issues and Best Practices
Edited by Jordi Trullen and Jaime Bonache

For more information about this series, please visit: www.routledge.com/
Routledge-Focus-on-Issues-in-Global-Talent-Management/book-series/
RFIGTM

Talent Management in Latin America
Pressing Issues and Best Practices

**Edited by Jordi Trullen and
Jaime Bonache**

 Routledge
Taylor & Francis Group

NEW YORK AND LONDON

First published 2021
by Routledge
605 Third Avenue, New York, NY 10158

and by Routledge
2 Park Square, Milton Park, Abingdon, Oxon, OX14 4RN

Routledge is an imprint of the Taylor & Francis Group, an informa business

Library of Congress Cataloging-in-Publication Data
Names: Trullen, Jordi, 1975- editor. | Bonache, Jaime, editor.
Title: Talent management in Latin America: pressing issues and
    best practices/edited by Jordi Trullen and Jaime Bonache.
Description: New York, NY: Routledge, 2021. | Series:
    Routledge focus on issues in global talent management |
    Includes bibliographical references and index.
Identifiers: LCCN 2021005248 (print) | LCCN 2021005249
    (ebook) | ISBN 9780367819903 (hardback) |
    ISBN 9781032046761 (paperback) | ISBN 9781003015918
    (ebook)
Subjects: LCSH: Personnel management—Latin America. |
    Human capital—Latin America—Management.
Classification: LCC HF5549.2.L29 T35 2021 (print) |
    LCC HF5549.2.L29 (ebook) | DDC 658.30098—dc23

LC record available at https://lccn.loc.gov/2021005248
LC ebook record available at https://lccn.loc.gov/2021005249

ISBN: 978-0-367-81990-3 (hbk)
ISBN: 978-1-032-04676-1 (pbk)
ISBN: 978-1-003-01591-8 (ebk)

Typeset in Times New Roman
by Apex CoVantage, LLC

To my favorite Brazilian, Ana Paula, and to our usual suspects, Gabriel and Tiago.

Jordi Trullen

To my favorite family Celia, little Jaime and Kleine Celia, and to those who inspire me to read and travel around the world.

Jaime Bonache

Contents

Contributors

Jaime Bonache is Professor of Management at University Carlos III of Madrid (Spain) and University Ramon Llull, ESADE (Spain). He has also been a Full Professor at Cranfield School of Management (UK). He has lived and worked in Canada, Spain, UK, and Germany. His research interest lies in Global Mobility, Cross-cultural Management, and Epistemology.

Antonio Carvalho Neto is Full Professor at Pontifical Catholic University of Minas Gerais, Brazil, where he lives. He was director of the Brazilian academy of management and currently is researcher at the CNPq (National Council). His research interests lie in industrial and labor relations, workforce diversity management, and the impact of new technologies on the labor market.

Wilson Aparecido Costa de Amorim is Associate Professor at University of São Paulo, Brazil, where he lives. He takes part of the advisory group of the CRANET (international HRM research network) and invited researcher at Fudan University (Shanghai—China). His research interests lie in industrial and labor relations, human resource management, and labor market.

Anabella Davila is Professor of Strategy, Strategic Human Resource Management, and Latin American Management at the EGADE Business School, Tecnologico de Monterrey, Mexico. Her research interests include human resource management, human development, and sustainability. Her work examines the social logic that governs Latin American organizations. Dr. Davila is a member of the National Researchers System in Mexico (Tier II).

Julián Darío Díaz Avendaño is a doctoral student at IAE Business School and Lecturer at Austral University (Argentina). He is an Industrial Engineer and holds an MBA from IAE Business School. Combining insights from organizational behavior and human resource management, his research interests include the dynamics of organizational identification, anti-identities, and their relationship with an organization's stakeholders.

Prof. **Luis Gómez Mejía** received his bachelor's master's degrees and PhD from the University of Minnesota. He is a Regents University Professor at Arizona State University. He has published more than 250 articles, with many of them in leading management journals. He has been in the top 1% most highly cited list in the Web of Science for the past eight years.

Michel Hermans is Associate Professor at IAE Business School of Austral University (Argentina). He holds a PhD from Cornell University's ILR School (United States) and master's and bachelor's degrees from the Rotterdam School of Management at Erasmus University (Netherlands). He conducts research at the intersection of Strategic Human Resource Management and International Business, focusing specifically on employee outcomes.

Milagros Molina has a degree in psychology and is Assistant Professor at Universidad Austral (FCE and FCB), Argentina. She teaches undergrad courses of Organizational Psychology and Organizational Development. She is research assistant focusing in projects around Family Business and Work Orientation. She has experience in vocational guidance to high school students.

Jacobo Ramirez is Assistant Professor of Latin American Business Development at Copenhagen Business School (CBS). Ramirez's main research interest is HRM and organizational strategy in fragile states and other complex institutional environments facing security risks, displacement, and social unrest. Jacobo Ramirez was born in Mexico and has lived and worked in Copenhagen since 2006.

Juan I. Sanchez is Professor and Knight-Ridder Byron Harless Eminent Scholar in Management at Florida International University in Miami. With over 100 refereed journal articles and more than 20 books, his work has been cited over 11,000 times. A five-time panelist of the National Academy of Sciences, he has served as associate editor and editorial board member of seven journals.

Lúcia Dos Santos Garcia is a master's student in the Graduate Program in Economics at the Federal University of Rio Grande do Sul, where she lives. She works in the Inter-Union Department of Statistics and Socioeconomic Studies (DIEESE), as a specialist in household surveys and the labor market. Her current research is on digital technology in the job market.

Anne-Marie Søderberg is Professor Emerita of Intercultural Communication and Cross-cultural Management (CCM) at Copenhagen Business
School, Denmark. Her research on CCM and HRM issues has been published in international management journals, and in books and edited
volumes such as "Global Collaboration: Intercultural Experiences and
Learning" (2012) and "Sage Handbook of Contemporary Cross-Cultural
Management" (2020).

Jordi Trullen is Associate Professor at Universitat Ramon Llull, ESADE
(Spain). He holds a PhD from Boston College (US). His research interests focus on the effective implementation of HRM policies in organizations and the role played by different actors, as well as on international
and comparative HRM. He is currently serving as an associate editor for
HRM/OB topics at Business Research Quarterly.

Prof. **Pedro Vázquez** (PhD) is Associate Professor at Universidad Austral (FCE & IAE Business School), Argentina. He teaches, consults,
and conducts research mainly on Governance and Family Business. He
has published in journals such as the *Journal of Business Ethics* and the
Journal of Family Business Strategy. He presides the Latin American
Chapter of IFERA (International Family Enterprise Research Academy).

Guillermo Wated is Professor of Psychology at Barry University in Miami,
Florida. He earned his MBA from the University of Miami and his PhD
in Industrial and Organizational Psychology from Florida International
University. His research program related to counterproductive behaviors
in organizations has generated publications in high-impact refereed journals including the *Journal of Business Ethics* and *Academy of Management Journal*.

1   Introduction

Jaime Bonache and Jordi Trullen

Half a century ago, the Uruguayan writer Eduardo Galeano asserted that *"as far as the world is concerned, America is nothing more than the United States: we inhabit, at most, a sub-America, a second-class America with a nebulous identification. It is Latin America, the region of open veins"* (Galeano, 1971). If we come to the present time and review the content of international manuals on human resource management, even those manuals most used and influential in Latin America, it is difficult not to agree with the above words by Galeano. In contrast to the huge amount we know about management problems in the US, where there is a wealth of research on the most varied determinants and effects of managing people in various ways, what we usually find in such manuals about the reality of human resources in Latin America is anecdotal and marginal.

We believe that this scarce attention and apparent lack of interest in managing people in Latin America is an error for two reasons—one quantitative and the other qualitative. Regarding the first, much objective data underlines the economic importance of the region: Latin America represents 14% of the world's land mass and covers some eight million square miles (Nicholls-Nixon, Castilla, Garcia, & Pesquera, 2011); the region has a gross domestic product of $5.7 trillion and a population of more than 650 million (World Bank, 2020a); it attracts 10.7% of world foreign direct investment (UNCTAD, 2020); and accounts for 6.5% of the world economy and 8.4% of the world population, with two countries, Brazil and Mexico, among the world's 20 largest economies. If only because of the substantial investment made by many companies in Latin America, it does not seem sensible to operate in this region blindly and without evidence that enables businesses to assess what they should—and should not do—in terms of managing people.

But there is another and more qualitative reason to study personnel issues in Latin America. As the Cuban writer Alejo Carpentier (1949, p. 67) wrote at the end of the 1940s: "In Latin America, the wonderful is found around every corner, in the disorder, in the picturesque images of our cities . . . in our nature . . . and also in our history." The first author has traveled extensively in the region, given many training courses, and worked on the ground with companies and organizations that have local economic interests. The second author has traveled to various Latin American countries, as well as taught and collaborated with several Brazilian colleagues. All this has helped us discover the truth of Carpentier's words. Latin America is indeed an exciting environment. But, it is also an especially complex and unstable region, which makes it a particularly interesting and challenging subject for research. Just over a decade ago, optimism was dominant. It was highlighted how, in a period of some 20 years, Latin America had changed from having highly unstable closed economies ruled by authoritarian rulers, to becoming more democratic (Santiso, 2007). The region has also seen the emergence of major multinational companies (known as multilatinas), which had become global players (AmericaEconomía, 2016). As we write these pages, however, that optimism (as so often in the past) has changed into deep concern about the economic and social situation of the region. Some of the countries mentioned as examples of economic miracles (such as Brazil and Chile) suffer the same socioeconomic difficulties faced by countries in other latitudes, and the populism that is causing so much damage to various societies in the 21st century seems to have found an especially fertile ground in many Latin American nations and governments.

A few examples will enable us to emphasize the qualitative interest of the region. In 2019 (before the start of the pandemic), the following events occurred: the president of Bolivia had to flee from the nation after being accused of electoral fraud; in Chile and Colombia, there were major social revolts driven by student protest against economic reforms; in Costa Rica, there was a prolonged strike in the health and educational sectors; in Ecuador, there were mass demonstrations against a rising fuel prices; in Haiti, there were several riots aimed at overthrowing the president; in Honduras, there were protests about election irregularities; in Paraguay, the government had to restructure after the covert renegotiation of a hydroelectric contract with Brazil was revealed; in Peru, there was an open struggle between the president and congress; while in Nicaragua, there was a violent confrontation between the government and a broad coalition of civil society, the Catholic Church, and the private sector (World Bank, 2020b). All these occurred without counting the continuing explosive situation in Venezuela and the subsequent migrant crisis. Social unrest is now compounded by the COVID-19 pandemic, which included more than 8.3 million cases and more than 310,000 deaths as of September 14, 2020 (BBC, 2020), and which, according to some recent estimates, could impoverish 25 million people in Argentina, Brazil, Mexico, and Colombia alone (El Pais, 30 August 2020).

How can we lead people and manage organizations in such a difficult and unstable environment? What can managers do to attract, retain, and motivate people when they are surrounded by anxiety and pain—with populations suffering because of the fall in economic activity, the COVID-19 pandemic, and social instability? What is influencing these managers and what impact do their decisions have on affected stakeholders such as employees and local community? In short, what makes the People Management in the region more efficient and/or legitimate and how are human resource problems experienced?

It is difficult to answer these types of questions supported by quality scientific research. HRM research on Latin America remains scarce and descriptive when compared with other world regions such as Asia. It is true that, in recent years, a number of publications in academic management journals have directly addressed the Latin American context (Aguilera, Ciravegna, Cuervo-Cazurra, & Gonzalez-Perez, 2017; Bianchi, Mingo, & Fernandez, 2018; Hermans et al., 2017; Husted & de Sousa-Filho, 2019; Mingo, Junkunc, & Morales, 2018). Nevertheless, these works do not usually specifically address human resources. There is a need for more literature that addresses in a rigorous manner the talent management problems experienced in Latin America.

However, we do not want to exaggerate either. To say that there are few rigorous studies on people management in Latin America does not mean that there are none. If the reader chooses to search the databases for a reliable source on the subject, he or she will be pleased to find their effort rewarded. Works on the subject written almost 15 years ago by Elvira and Davila (2005) and Davila and Elvira (2009) stand out. These works offer an excellent conceptual framework for analyzing the implications that certain dominant regional work values (such as benevolent paternalism, personal contact, and popular traditions) have on the design, implementation, and results of specific human resource policies in Latin America. These works also indicate the need to have a good knowledge of the Latin American sociocultural environment, and not to uncritically apply frameworks and solutions from other countries (and especially, the Anglo-Saxon world).

This rejection of the simple importation into Latin America of "prefabricated" models of progress has been discussed by other authors, including the writer Carlos Fuentes, who with great subtlety and depth, has written memorable pages analyzing the sociocultural context of the region. For this Mexican author, there is a long Latin American tradition of venerating ideas from Europe and the US that have not always translated into substantial improvements for the continent. Culturally, independent Spanish America turned its back on its black and indigenous heritage in the 19th century and understood it as "barbaric." Subsequently, there was a rejection of everything Spanish, combined with great admiration for the US, and especially for France, as the world's cradles of progress. It was the time of Auguste Comte's positivist philosophy, according to which "human history developed in predictable and universally valid stages" (Fuentes, 1998, p. 425). A typical assumption was that the new Latin American nations could also become modern nations if they closely followed certain steps based on French and American experiences. This uncritical and xenocentric vision ended with negative consequences. While the elites imitated "French" and "American" tastes in areas such as consumption, clothing, architecture, political, social, and economic ideas, they were unable to apply the working models of these countries (which were perceived as straitjackets that were poorly adapted to Latin American cultural idiosyncrasies). Latin America thus became a source of raw material exports, but without generating for itself the necessary capital for investment and savings.

Analyzing the extent to which initiatives from "outside" the Latin American environment also work in this context is a key issue for empirical research. In fact, this is what we did in our own work when testing the typical universalist and culturalist visions in human resource management (Bonache, Trullen, & Sanchez, 2012). However, the way in which we addressed this subject (i.e. our methodological approach) was the typical and dominant approach used in intercultural management—but it is not the only possible approach. Let us clarify this point a little further to see what new research opportunities exist in this field, as well as what this book intends to contribute.

Providing a vision around the management challenges within a given region can ideally be done from two epistemological perspectives: positivist or interpretative (Szkudlarek, Romani, Caprar, & Osland, 2020; Bonache, 2020). The first approach is the most common and is adopted by Davila and Elvira, and is also the perspective we followed in our own work mentioned earlier. Based on the assumption that there is a social world independent of the researcher (in this case, the Latin American sociocultural world with its own management practices), this approach identifies regularities between variables of interest (such as relations between certain cultural values, HR practices, and behavioral outcomes) as well as "boundary conditions" that specify in which situations such regularities are most likely to occur (Donaldson, 2003; Sackman, 2020). This perspective differs from the constructivist or interpretivist perspective that focuses on understanding social phenomena from the point of view (or interpretation) of the various groups involved (Gertsen & Zølner, 2020). Although constructivist studies are increasingly influential and common in the field of intercultural management (Szkudlarek et al., 2020), it is unfortunately difficult to find studies on HR in Latin America from that perspective (indeed, we have not managed to find any). Such studies, by putting to rest the assumptions we normally hold about a given area and studying reality from a local point of view, would enable us to reveal specific (and possibly new and different) ways of looking at events in Latin America. Such studies may help generate more socially relevant research, and it would be extremely rewarding if any of the readers of this introduction take up the challenge of conducting that type of work.

When Professor Ibraiz Tarique, the editor of this collection, commissioned this book from us, our first idea was to prepare a manual about the reality of human resources in Latin America from the two perspectives mentioned earlier. However, the lack of constructivist studies led us to dismiss that idea. What then could we do? We decided to explore two other options. One of these was deductive: starting from a general index of topics to be covered and inviting various authors to write the chapters. A book organized in this way would undoubtedly be excellent. However, given the lack of data on most of the potential topics, it would run the serious risk of importing data and conceptual frameworks from other environments—and thus, the text would be constructed on very weak empirical pillars. We were thus left with a more inductive option. This consisted in carefully reviewing the recent scientific production on human resources in Latin America and identifying the issues and authors. This path would enable us to discover, without a priori frameworks or preconceived ideas, the topics and factors that are especially relevant to the Latin American scientific community. This is how the book came to be written. It includes chapters focused on factors or variables found in the general Latin American context: such as populism and unproductive behavior (Wated & Sanchez; Chapter 2); or informality and deregulation of the labor market (Amorim, Neto, and Garcia, Chapter 3). Other chapters analyze how specific human resource problems are approached in a Latin American context: such as the attraction of local talent (Ramirez and Søderberg, Chapter 4); or career management in family firms (Vazquez, Gómez Mejía and Molina; Chapter 5). Finally, there are two chapters analyzing how well-known human resources initiatives in other latitudes are understood and implemented in Latin America: such as socially responsible HRM (Davila, Chapter 6) or high-performance work systems (Hermans and Díaz Avendaño, Chapter 7). A simple glance at the list of chapters reveals that the book does not cover all the potentially important topics, but that all the topics included are important.

We will conclude by saying something about the work process that has made this book possible. After deciding the direction we wanted to take with the book, and carefully reviewing what has been published in the area over the past few years, we made a list of the ideal authors. Some of the authors were good friends, but others we had never met. We were pleased that everyone we invited to join the project chose to accept. From then on, the only priority was to collaborate with each other so as not to disappoint the publisher, authors, and potential readers. In this context, we recall what one of the few writers who worked in collaboration, the Argentinean Jorge Luis Borges, wrote about the success of his writings with his compatriot Bioy Casares:

> *I have been often asked how to write collaboratively. I think it requires the joint abandonment of the self, of vanity, and perhaps of courtesy. Collaborators must forget about themselves and think only in terms of the work.*
>
> *(Jorge Luis Borges, 1999; Autobiography, pp. 121)*

That is what we have tried to do in this book: think only in terms of the work. We hope that the result will bring readers some of the joy we experienced when discovering how much we can learn about managing people in Latin America.

References

Aguilera, R. V., Ciravegna, L., Cuervo-Cazurra, A., & Gonzalez-Perez, M. A. 2017. Multilatinas and the internationalization of Latin American firms. *Journal of World Business*, 52(4): 447–460.

AmericaEconomia. 2016. *Ranking multilatinas 2016*. Retrieved from http://rankings.americaeconomia.com/2016/multilatinas/ranking/

BBC News. 2020. *Coronavirus: What are the numbers out of Latin America?* Retrieved from www.bbc.com/news/world-latin-america-52711458

Bianchi, C., Mingo, S., & Fernandez, V. 2018. Strategic management in Latin America: Challenges in a changing world. *Journal of Business Research*. https://doi.org/10.1016/j.jbusres.2018.10.022

Bonache, J. 2020. The challenge of using a 'non-positivist' paradigm and getting through the peer-review process. *Human Resource Management Journal*, 1–12. https://doi.org/10.1111/1748-8583.12319

Bonache, J., Trullen, J., & Sanchez, J. I. 2012. Managing cross-cultural differences: Testing human resource models in Latin America. *Journal of Business Research*, 65: 1773–1781.

Borges, J. L. 1999. *Autobiografía*. Madrid: Ed. Ateneo.

Carpentier, A. 2002/1949. *El reino de este mundo: Los pasos perdidos*. Madrid: Siglo XXI.

Davila, A., & Elvira, M. M. 2009. *Best human resource management practices in Latin America*. Oxford: Routledge.

Donaldson, L. 2003. Organization theory as a positivist science. In H. Tsoukas & C. Knudsen (Eds.), *The Oxford handbook of organization theory* (pp. 39–62). Oxford: Oxford University Press.

El Pais. 2020. *Cuatro meses, cuatro países, cuatro respuestas.* Retrieved January 21, 2021, from https://elpais.com/economia/2020-08-29/cuatro-meses-cuatro-paises-cuatro-respuestas.html.

Elvira, M. M., & Davila, A. 2005. *Managing human resources in Latin America: An agenda for international leaders.* Oxford: Routledge.

Fuentes, C. 1998. *El espejo enterrado.* Madrid: Editorial Taurus.

Galeano, E. 1971. *Las Venas Abiertas de América Latina.* Ciudad de México: Siglo Veintiuno Editores.

Gertsen, M. C., & Zølner, M. 2020. Interpretive approaches to culture. In B. Szkudlarek, L. Romani, D. Caprar, & J. Osland (Eds.), *The Sage handbook of contemporary cross-cultural management.* London: Sage Publications.

Hermans, M., Newburry, W., Alvarado-Vargas, M. J., Baldo, C. M., Borda, A., Durán-Zurita, E. G., & Olivas-Lujan, M. R. 2017. Attitudes towards women's career advancement in Latin America: The moderating impact of perceived company international proactiveness. *Journal of International Business Studies*, 48(1): 90–112.

Husted, B. W., & de Sousa-Filho, J. M. 2019. Board structure and environmental, social, and governance disclosure in Latin America. *Journal of Business Research*, 102: 220–227.

Mingo, S., Junkunc, M., & Morales, F. 2018. The interplay between home and host country institutions in an emerging market context: Private equity in Latin America. *Journal of World Business*, 53(5): 653–667.

Nicholls-Nixon, C. L., Castilla, J. A. D., Garcia, J. S., & Pesquera, M. R. 2011. Latin America management research: Review, synthesis, and extension. *Journal of Management*, 37: 1178–1227.

Sackman, S. A. 2020. Culture in cross-cultural management: Its seminal contributors from a positivist perspective. In B. Szkudlarek, L. Romani, D. Caprar, & J. Osland (Eds.), *The Sage handbook of contemporary cross-cultural management.* London: Sage Publications.

Santiso, J. 2007. *Latin America's political economy of the possible: Beyond good revolutionaries and free-marketeers.* Cambridge, MA: MIT Press.

Szkudlarek, B., Romani, L., Caprar, D., & Osland, J. 2020. *The Sage handbook of contemporary cross-cultural management.* London: Sage Publications.

UNCTAD. 2020. *World investment report.* Geneva, Switzerland: United Nations Conference on Trade and Development.

World Bank. 2020a. *Data center.* Retrieved January 21, 2021, from https://data.worldbank.org/region/latin-america-and-caribbean.

World Bank. 2020b. *Semiannual report of the Latin America and Caribbean region: The economy in the time of Covid-19.* Retrieved January 21, 2021, from https://openknowledge.worldbank.org/bitstream/handle/10986/33555/9781464815706.pdf.

2 Political Populism-to-Work Spillover in Latin America

Implications for Human Resources Management

Guillermo Wated and Juan I. Sanchez

Introduction

The first quarter of the 21st century has witnessed a rebirth of populism around the World. The designation of the word *populism* as the Cambridge Dictionary 2017's *Word of the Year* based on search frequency and search spikes attests to the renewed interest in this phenomenon (Cambridge University Press, 2017). We define populism as a political movement that promotes restitution in favor of groups that have allegedly become the victims of both elites and those perceived to be favored by such elites (Conniff, 1982; de la Torre, 2000; Dornbusch & Edwards, 1989; Gidron & Hall, 2017; Moffitt & Tormey, 2014; Mudde, 2004; Stavrakakis, Kioupkiolis, Katsambekis, Nikisianis, & Siomos, 2016; Wejnert, 2014; Woods, 2014). At the core of populism lies an acute sense of social identification with a so-called group of victims whose interests juxtapose those of the *elites* (or those of other groups allegedly favored by the elites).

Populist movements either have a strong presence or hold political power in nations as diverse as Australia, Austria, Bolivia, Brazil, Ecuador, Egypt, France, Germany, Holland, Hungary, Italy, Mexico, Nicaragua, Poland, Spain, Turkey, US, Venezuela, and Zambia (de la Torre, 2015; Moffitt, 2017; Inglehart & Norris, 2016). However, Latin America enjoys probably the world's "*most enduring and prevalent populist tradition*" (Mudde & Kaltwasser, 2013) that started almost a century ago in the aftermath of the 1929 Great Depression under leaders such as Lázaro Cárdenas in México, Juan Perón in Argentina, Getulio Vargas in Brazil, and José María Velasco Ibarra in Ecuador (Cachanosky & Padilla, 2018).

Although populism is a widely studied phenomenon (e.g., Cannon, 2009; de la Torre, 2017; Oxendine, 2019), a majority of research has focused on its political and economic aspects while overlooking the potential management implications for organizations operating in a populist-dominated sociopolitical environment. We argue that populist movements in Latin America and possibly elsewhere have the potential to produce drastic changes in employee attitudes and subsequent behavior, which are likely to spill over to the work context and impact organizations. These new circumstances demand equally radical changes in the way organizations manage their human resources.

In this chapter, we propose a theoretical model that aims to explain how populist-dominated sociopolitical environments have the potential to provoke spillover effects on employee and organizational outcomes. Given our purpose of elucidating the management implications of populism, the key characteristic of populism for us is not the ideology or political sign of the populist leader in question, but the fact that populism, regardless of its political sign, triggers a psychological process of social identification that leads to the development of an entitlement attitude whereby employees are likely to reduce their performance contributions. In fact, even though very visible left-leaning leaders such as the late Hugo Chávez from Venezuela are often at the helmet of populist movements, the ideology of populist leaders runs the gamut from the far left to the extreme right of the political spectrum (de la Torre, 2017; Gott, 2011; Moffitt & Tormey, 2014). Regardless of their ideology, the primary message of populist leaders is their identification with the alleged victims' unfair treatment and exclusion while advocating a political agenda of restitution that has the potential to revert such perceived injustices.

Prior research focusing on the sociopolitical roots of populism notwithstanding, virtually no authors have attempted to elaborate on the process through which populism might spill over to the work context. We maintain that organizations operating in a sociopolitical environment dominated by populism, and populist leaders should be aware of the potential spillover effects on how employees approach their jobs. Indeed, the phenomenon of populism is so pervasive in certain societies that spillover effects beyond the political arena to the work context are expected. Specifically, a populist-charged sociopolitical environment is likely to trigger an individual psychological process of social identification that will ultimately shape employee attitudes and behavior at work. In fact, the deep social divide that characterizes societies like those in Latin America, together with the collectivistic imperative to classify individuals in the ingroup versus outgroup membership categories, are likely to exacerbate the rise of populism as well as its influence on other life spheres like the manner in which individuals behave at work (Gomez, Kirkman, & Shapiro, 2000; Stromquist, 2004; Tajfel, 1974). Organizations that ignore this reality are condemned to continue using obsolete human resource management models that cannot meet the new demands of employees, who are undoubtedly influenced by a sociopolitical environment in which populism exerts a pervasive influence on not only nonwork but also work aspects of life.

In the sections that follow, we elaborate a theoretical model (see Figure 2.1) grounded on a cross-fertilization of the following theories: social identity theory, paternalistic leadership theory, and the attitude-formation theory of reasoned action. The theoretical grounds of each one of the links in our model are reviewed in detail in the next sections, but the following constitutes a brief synopsis of our model.

Link 1 explains why many current and potential employees living in a populist-dominated socioeconomic environment identify themselves as members of a victimized class of individuals. The strength of this link would be exacerbated for individuals living in cultures dominated by collectivistic norms that encourage categorizations of others as either ingroup or outgroup members. As described in Link 2 of our model, the individuals' social identification as members of the victims' group leads them to harbor a series of entitlement beliefs that they feel they deserve by virtue of their perceived social identity. However, Link 3 shows that employees do not necessarily develop an entitlement attitude that is consistent with their beliefs because even though they deem their beliefs desirable, they might remain unconvinced about the feasibility of turning such beliefs into realities. The emergence of a populist leader plays a key role in the extent to which individuals begin to believe in the likelihood of their entitlements becoming realities. We draw from paternalistic leadership theory to highlight the two critical dimensions of a populist leader, namely authoritarianism and benevolence, which in our view have a determining effect on the perceived likelihood that desirable entitlement beliefs will turn into realities. As predicted by the attitude-formation theory of reasoned action, we postulate in Link 3 that the combination of the desirability of entitlement beliefs provoked by the employees' identification as members of a victimized group, combined with the perceived likelihood that an emerging populist leader would turn those entitlements into realities, will foster an attitude of psychological entitlement. Link 4, which is the last link in our model, anticipates that those entering the work context holding a psychological entitlement attitude are likely compelled to diminish their work performance contributions. However, the strength of Link 4 will be attenuated (i.e., moderated), when organizations put in place a series of human resource practices informed by merit-driven and affirmative action principles that should ameliorate the otherwise negative work behaviors that an attitude of psychological entitlement is likely to bring to the workplace in a sociopolitical environment dominated by populist forces.

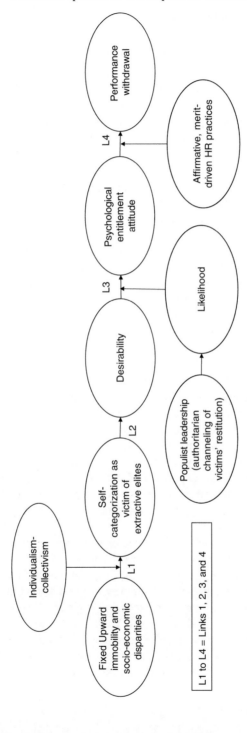

Figure 2.1 A Model of Populism Spillover to Work

Theoretical Background

Link 1: Developing the Social Identity of a Victim

Several theoretical models have attempted to pinpoint the antecedents of populism. For instance, Cannon (2009) stated that populism is driven by political, social, and economic factors such as weak governmental institutions, economic failures, and the pressure of modernization forces like globalization. Besides economic factors, Gidron and Hall (2017) added the impact of cultural factors such as changes in value systems that people use to interpret the world around them. Furthermore, Oxendine (2019) proposed a model that includes both macro (e.g., economic inequality, political, and economic dysfunction) and individual (e.g., status anxiety, low confidence in government) level antecedents of populist support.

The surge of populism is often explained by its implicit promise to resolve historic social inequalities that seem insurmountable in certain societies. Indeed, some authors opine that the renaissance of populism has actually bolstered both democracy and economic development in Latin America (e.g., Canovan, 1999; Laclau, 1977; Laurence, 2016; Stavrakakis & Katsambekis, 2014; Stiglitz, 2003). For instance, some have argued that free higher education became a constitutional right under Hugo Chávez's government in Venezuela, which, according to these authors, brought increased access, elevated standards, and a variety of educational opportunities (Muhr & Verger, 2006). Similarly, Cannon (2009) asserts that populism created policies of redistribution that benefited marginalized sectors in the society, thereby increasing their democratic participation and popular empowerment in Venezuela. Furthermore, an empirical study commissioned by the British newspaper *The Guardian* that assessed populist governments from 40 countries around the world concluded that populism actually reduces income inequality and has a modest yet positive effect on voter turnover (Hawkins, 2019). In short, the state-owned formulas often implicit in populist movements continue to be presented in some quarters as a solution to overcome chronic social inequalities.

As it is often the case, when state-owned versus private enterprises are compared (Wated, Sanchez, & Gomez, 2008), mixed evidence concerning the pros and cons of populism seem to coexist. For instance, many regard the comeback of populism in Latin America as a disruptive political force that has curtailed freedom and democracy in general (Coronel, 2006a; de la Torre, 2015; Houle & Kenny, 2018; Mudde & Kaltwasser, 2013; Panizza, 2009). For instance, the populist government initiated by Hugo Chávez in Venezuela has been accused of eliminating the separation of powers by concentrating power in the executive, repressing political rivals, and exercising top-down control of civil society (de la Torre, 2017). Moreover, upon his first election in 2007, Ecuador's former populist leader Rafael Correa was accused of using his political power through a referendum to suspend the powers of Congress alleging corruption, and replacing it with a Constituent Assembly (Selçuk, 2016). The Assembly drafted a new constitution, later also ratified by referendum, that enhanced the concentration of power in the executive, restricted freedom of the press, and extended the presidential term to two consecutive four-year terms (Madrid, Hunter, & Weyland, 2010).

Houle and Kenny (2018) empirically assessed the performance of left and right-leaning populist governments from Argentina, Bolivia, Brazil, Colombia, Ecuador, Haiti, Nicaragua, Paraguay, Peru, and Venezuela from 1982 to 2012 in regard to the rule of law, elimination of executive power constraints (the erosion of horizontal checks and balances), judicial independence from the executive branch, and voters' participation in presidential elections. The authors concluded that populism reduced executive constraints, the rule of law, and judicial independence.

Critics have also pointed out the economic drawbacks of populism. Economic reforms such as nationalization of public enterprises and price controls promoted by populist leaders are said to create social expectations that are hard if not impossible to meet, unintentionally provoking disastrous levels of inflation and capital flight out of the country (Rodríguez Braun, 2012). For instance, the capital flight from Venezuela under Nicolás Maduro's presidency reached an estimate of $19,718 billion during the first nine months of 2019, which is the highest figure recorded in Venezuela since 1997 (Morgan, 2019). Furthermore, Sánchez (2019) reported that inflation in Venezuela was 10 million percent in 2019. Houle and Kenny (2018) stated that income inequality (i.e., the extent to which wealth is concentrated in a group of already financially well-off individuals) is not significantly better in countries ruled by populist rather than non-populist parties.

In a more recent example, leaders ranging from the center-right to the far left have used the coronavirus pandemic to justify the implementation of authoritarian measures that further inhibit democracy in Latin America (Kurmanaev, 2020). For instance, the current president of Venezuela, Nicolás Maduro, silenced journalists, and opposition leaders by detaining them and raiding their homes alleging that they had falsely questioned the Venezuelan government's coronavirus figures. And in Bolivia, the caretaker government of Jeanine Áñez alluded to the pandemic to justify postponing the elections and threatening to block the main opposition candidate from running for president.

In this chapter, however, we neither focus on the economic merits (or drawbacks) of populism nor do we take an ideological position in favor of or against populist movements. Instead, we focus on the psychological process that a populism-dominated context triggers, as well as on the potential spillover of such a process to the individual's work sphere.

We suggest that the same deep social disparities allegedly targeted by the reforms advocated by populist leaders act as a catalyst of a psychological process that has the potential to spill over to the organizational arena by shaping attitudes and performance at work. However, we maintain that the perception of current and prior institutional and economic failures cannot solely explain the phenomenon of populism. Indeed, societal norms that draw clear-cut distinctions among classes thereby restricting access to tangible and intangible resources also drive those individuals to initiate a psychological process of social identification in which they categorize themselves as members of an allegedly victimized group. Members of this group share the belief that they are indeed the victims of an extractive elite that accumulates and distributes resources and opportunities in a manner that presumably excludes or at least punishes them (Conniff, 1982; de la Torre, 2000; Dornbusch & Edwards, 1989; Gidron & Hall, 2017; Moffitt & Tormey, 2014; Mudde, 2004; Stavrakakis et al., 2016; Wejnert, 2014; Woods, 2014).

The potential to trigger this type of social identification is huge in Latin America, where class definitions often proceed along the lines of visible characteristics such as race and ethnicity, which severely limit peoples' perceived access to resources and opportunities (Stromquist, 2004). In fact, with the exception of Sub-Saharan Africa, Latin America is the region with the greatest inequality in most economic indicators such as income, education, and health outcomes in the world (De Ferranti, Perry, Ferreira, & Walton, 2004).

Social inequalities in Latin America are indeed deeply entrenched in group-based characteristics. These inequalities date back to colonial times, where indigenous groups and African slaves were used to meet the European settlers' labor demands in the system of "encomienda" or royal licensing to exploit the land on behalf of the crown (De Ferranti et al., 2004). These inequalities have persisted through time, and despite the great diversity found in Latin America today, the notion that those who are white fare better than those who are mestizo, Indian or black is, according to Stromquist (2004), deeply entrenched in the culture. Furthermore, it has been argued that post-independence political and economic institutions have reinforced unequal distribution of wealth, education, human capital and political influence along ethnic and racial lines beyond those of colonial times (De Ferranti et al., 2004). Poverty and unequal access to education and capital limit people's access to goods and services, social mobility, and ultimately strengthen their sense of belongingness to a social category with rather limited perceived ability to control their own future (Kabeer, 1998).

Social identity theory (Tajfel, 1974) proposes that individuals have a tendency to define themselves according to group membership (i.e., ingroup or "like us" and outgroup or "unlike us" members), and that this categorization defines these individuals' social world. For instance, "nationality" creates an ingroup (e.g., countrymen and women) and an outgroup (e.g., foreigners). Similarly, we propose that the aforementioned social, political, and economic disparities trigger a psychological process in which marginalized individuals categorized themselves as victims of extractive elites, thereby creating an ingroup (the marginalized) sense of belongingness defined by its counterpart the outgroup (the elite). We postulate that the relatively high levels of societal collectivism in Latin America will exacerbate the effects of social disparities on social identification, because differences in individualism–collectivism have been found to taint evaluations of outgroup members, who are generally seen in a less favorable light by collectivists (Gomez et al., 2000).

Link 2: The Structure of the Psychological Entitlement Attitude

Consistent with social identity theory, we expect members of the ingroup to adopt the beliefs of the group in which they have categorized themselves. Fishbein and Ajzen (2010) suggested that beliefs "are acquired in daily encounters with the real world" (224). Therefore, members of the outgroup will share a series of beliefs that reflect their economic, social, and political aspirations such as the belief to have a certain degree of opportunity to access capital, decrease inequality, follow a life of their own choosing or have social mobility.

The theory of reasoned action (Ajzen & Fishbein, 1980; Fishbein & Ajzen, 1975), and its successor the theory of planned behavior (Ajzen, 1985, 1987), stated that attitudes are shaped by the beliefs that people endorse. Attitudes refer to a person's positive or negative evaluation about performing a behavior (Ajzen & Fishbein, 1980). Consequently, we propose that the aforementioned group-shared beliefs will impact the ingroup members' attitudes toward their social's world, in particular, their attitudes toward entitlement.

Entitlement beliefs are rooted in the distribution of resources in society (Campbell, Bonacci, Shelton, Exline, & Bushman, 2004). From tax breaks and social welfare to access to education and grades, individuals exchange their skills or resources for some form of compensation or privilege (Tiwari, 2007). Nevertheless, in societies in which inequality is as pervasive as it is in Latin America, these exchanges fall short. In fact, poverty has been conceived as the failure to meet basic needs for the marginalized such as economic, social, cultural, and human rights (de Gaay Fortman, 2006). Therefore, we define attitude toward entitlement as the marginalized individuals' positive evaluations of behaviors that will restitute perceived fairness to the members of their victimized group, e.g., receiving a fixed salary that covers their basic needs regardless of their performance level or engaging in strikes to compel employers to increase their salaries.

And yet the theory of planned behavior distinguishes between two dimensions of every belief, desirability, and likelihood that, combined, form an attitude (Ajzen, 1985, 1987). Desirability refers to an individuals' subjective evaluation of the belief (e.g., "reducing social inequality is desired"), whereas likelihood illustrates the subjective evaluation that a particular belief is obtainable (e.g., "reducing social inequality is within my reach"). Therefore, the prediction of whether or not individuals holding entitlement attitudes will engage in behaviors that are consistent with their attitude depends not only on how much these individuals desire beliefs such as social justice but also on how likely they believe social justice is to become a reality.

Link 3: The Role of the Populist Leader as a Catalyst of Entitlement Attitudes

We propose that the emergence of a populist leader acts as a catalyst for the beliefs of the marginalized to shape their entitlement attitude. More specifically, a populist leader should be instrumental in convincing those who have classified themselves as members of the marginalized group that their desires for restitution, fair access, and equal opportunities are now achievable, thereby increasing the likelihood of their beliefs turning into realities. As predicted by the theory of reasoned action (Ajzen & Fishbein, 1980; Fishbein & Ajzen, 1975), the perceived likelihood that their beliefs might soon become realities will open up the doors to acting on their already desired beliefs hence enabling their entitlement attitude.

The perception that a populist leader would help convert desirable beliefs into likely realities should be facilitated by a populist leader, who displays a paternalistic leadership style. Paternalistic leadership combines two separate dimensions of leadership, namely authoritarianism and benevolence, which together create "a style that combines strong discipline and authority with fatherly benevolence" (Farh & Cheng, 2000, p. 91). Although a majority of research on paternalistic leadership has focused on Asian samples (Takeuchi, Wang, & Farh, 2020), paternalistic leadership is well suited to the Latin American context (Martinez, 2005).

Research on paternalistic leadership suggests that the leader's benevolent stance as a social exemplar of the group reduces the otherwise negative effects of authoritarianism on followers' outcomes (Tian & Sanchez, 2017). That is, populist leaders often portray themselves as the benevolent representatives of the marginalized/oppressed, sharing their values and beliefs, and whose primary role is to vigorously defend their interests by cracking down on the sources of their problems through their authoritarian style (Ernst, 2017). This morally benevolent stance as a group exemplar seems to buy the populist leader a license to behave in autocratic and even despotic ways, especially when making decisions that allegedly run against the outgroup's interests. For instance, both former Venezuelan President Hugo Chavez and Brazil's current president Jair Bolsonaro capitalized on public frustration with endemic corruption to hurl their political campaigns promising to fight against the elites but at the same time helping those in need (Coronel, 2006b; Preissler Iglesia, Viotti Beck, & Adghirni, 2020). Similarly, US President Donald Trump occasionally portrayed himself as the defender of the people against elites that allegedly do little or nothing to protect the country against the interests of outsiders like foreign nations and immigrants (Ernst, 2017). We propose that this style of paternalistic-populist leadership influences followers' behavior by giving them the sense that their long-desired beliefs can now turn into realities, hence giving them the courage to enact behaviors consistent with their new entitlement attitudes.

Link 4: Managing Human Resources in a Populism-Dominated Environment

A political environment tainted by populism has the potential to create several challenges for managers in Latin America. Previously, we proposed that populist leaders will enable their followers to not only form but also act upon their entitlement attitudes, i.e., their psychological entitlement toward resources, access, and opportunities that were allegedly denied to members of their social group in the past. Psychological entitlement refers to a sense that one not only deserves more but it is also entitled to more than others, which can eventually have a pervasive, destructive impact on behavior (Campbell et al., 2004). And in fact, psychological entitlement has been documented to have a detrimental effect in the workplace. For instance, Harvey and Martinko (2008) found that employees' psychological entitlement was positively associated with reduced job satisfaction, increased levels of conflict with supervision, and turnover intention. Similarly, we propose that employees who identify themselves as members of a marginalized group of victims and whose entitlement attitudes have been activated by the presence of a populist leader are likely to engage in one or more forms of performance withdrawal. For example, psychological entitlement may lead employees to perceive that their employers "owe them" since employers are presumably seen as controlled by the exploiting elite responsible for their disadvantages in society. Therefore, they would expect the organization to compensate them for their work regardless of their job performance as a form of deserved restitution. These ideas are consistent with reports suggesting that corporate social expenses of state-owned firms have skyrocketed immediately after populist leaders' access to power (La Nación, 2007).

Still another consequence of an entitlement attitude might be an increase in the number of transgressions and challenges to the status quo and authority figures, which should collide with traditional norms of high power distance in Latin American society. Power distance is a cultural value gauging the degree of tolerance for power and status differences within an organization (Hofstede, 1980). Hofstede's (1980) findings suggest that Latin American organizations tend to be high on power distance, i.e., managers in Latin American organizations are likely to demand obedience from subordinates and consider themselves of higher status than their subordinates. The marginalized employees' heightened sense of entitlement might encourage them to challenge the existing power structure of their employer organization, which is likely to be perceived as an inherited by-product of social inequalities deeply entrenched in society. This power struggle within the organization can provoke conflict, which has been documented to negatively impact performance (e.g., De Dreu & Weingart, 2003; Rahim, Antonioni, Krumov, & Ilieva, 2000).

Entitled employees might also be less likely to engage in organizational citizenship behavior (OCB). OCB is an aspect of human behavior at work where employees choose to go beyond the core requirements of the job while contributing to overall organizational effectiveness (MacKenzie, Posakoff, & Fetter, 1991; Organ, 1988). Among its antecedents are job satisfaction, organizational commitment, perceptions of justice, and the quality of the relationship with supervisors (Hoffman, Blair, Meriac, & Woehr, 2007). According to our model, entitled employees probably lack the motivation needed to engage in OCB as they perceive the organization to be undeserving of their extra effort. After all, in their view, the organization is an extension of an elite that has marginalized them from society and kept them from accessing the resources to which they are entitled.

Adapting Affirmative Action Practices to a Populist Environment

As presented earlier, a populist-dominated political environment creates specific managerial challenges for the human resources function, whose role is to balance micro and macro environmental forces in order to help the organization implement practices that are critical for its strategy (Gomez & Sanchez, 2005). Because management practices are socially constructed and therefore partly influenced by political culture (Dobbin, Sutton, Meyer, & Scott, 1993), the challenges presented by a populist political environment call for HR practices aimed at channeling employees' entitlement attitudes in a manner conducive to positive evaluations of the organizations they work for (Cohen-Charash & Spector, 2001).

As a first step, organizations should consider the creation and implementation of corporate policies informed by equal opportunity that eliminate unfair discrimination based on race, ethnicity, social class, or tradition. This includes the implementation of merit-driven staffing and performance evaluation practices that facilitate similarly merit-based employment decisions. There is evidence suggesting that equal employment opportunity policies stimulate fairness in organizations by fostering the creation of HR practices that treat all workers as ambitious and achievement-oriented (Dobbin et al., 1993). Furthermore, there is well-documented evidence suggesting that perceptions of fairness are positively related to job performance, job satisfaction, intention not to quit, and team performance (e.g., Cohen-Charash & Spector, 2001; Whitman, Caleo, Carpenter, Horner, & Bernerth, 2012).

Still another step that organizations may consider is to initiate affirmative action programs targeting individuals from underprivileged groups. Affirmative action refers to practices that organizations implement to address past discrimination against certain demographic groups (Kravitz, 2008). Affirmative action aims to remedy historical discrimination and barriers to access jobs that used to be off-limits to certain classes of individuals. In the US, affirmative action is not a quota system requiring organizations to hire or promote unqualified employees (Bennett-Alexander, 1990). That is, social group membership should be weighed only after job qualifications that merit the hiring or promotion have been met (Pettigrew & Martin, 1987). In Latin America, the implementation of merit-based affirmative action plans might allow members of allegedly victimized groups to gain access to positions historically earmarked for members of the elite. These programs may include extra recruitment efforts from traditionally underrepresent groups in Latin American society such as indigenous tribes as well as training and development programs that target the development of the required KSAOs (knowledge, skills, abilities, and other characteristics) among those belonging to underrepresented groups.

Our endorsement of affirmative action programs in the Latin American context notwithstanding, much research on how these programs should be conceived and implemented is needed. For instance, allowing self-categorizations of individuals as members of an underprivileged group might not always be reasonable. The means and potentially verifiable criteria through which the social categorizations that define underprivileged groups should proceed warrant further research. These criteria might very well vary from country to country as a function of differences in how social, racial, ethnic, and gender factors have historically been dealt with in each country. For instance, acknowledging the large African heritage of the country, Banco de Santander Brazil has pledged to increase the number of black employees to at least 30% of their workforce by 2021 (Banco de Santander, 2020).

When considering the implementation of affirmative action plans, caution should be exercised to avoid the stigmatization of those who are intended to benefit from them. Since its onset in the US close to 60 years ago, controversy has surrounded the implementation of affirmative action plans due in part to an erroneous assumption that affirmative action entails quotas or even preferential treatment based upon factors other than merit, thereby exacerbating perceptions of distributive and procedural injustice among nonbeneficiaries in organizations (Crosby & VanDeVeer, 2000; Kravitz & Platania, 1993; Kravitz et al., 1997). These perceptions have stigmatized the targets of affirmative action plans as incompetent and not deserving of job allotments or promotions (Heilman, Simon, & Repper, 1987; Niemann & Dovidio, 2005), which in turn has a detrimental impact on their job satisfaction and performance (Garcia, Erskine, Hawn, & Casmay, 1981; Harris, Lievens, & Van Hoye, 2004; Leslie, Mayer, & Kravitz, 2014). Consider for instance the case of Malaysia, where affirmative action programs have provided certain minority groups upward mobility into higher levels at the expense of stigmatization of their beneficiaries as incompetent (Kong, 2014).

Therefore, it is imperative that perceptions of fairness in the implementation of affirmative action plans in Latin American organizations learn from prior mistakes made elsewhere. For instance, corporate affirmative action and equal employment policies need to be properly communicated to all members of the organization by emphasizing the importance of finding qualified candidates and promoting workers from all segments of society to foster support for affirmative action programs (Leslie et al., 2014). Moreover, the recruitment, hiring, and promotion efforts should be positively framed and highlight the potential talent and qualifications of workers targeted by affirmative action plans. Indeed, it might be helpful to incorporate the lessons learned from other nations that have developed affirmative action policies in recent times like South Africa, where the courts have ruled that the composition of the economically active population at both the regional and national levels must be first considered before the social groups are defined—these groups typically capture the country's history (e.g., black African, colored, Indian, white) (Mullingan, 2020).

In short, although we are not suggesting a moratorium on the implementation of equal employment and affirmative action plans in Latin America, research is needed to better understand and anticipate how such programs may best adapt to a Latin American context. Future studies should first uncover the antecedents of employees' attitudes toward such plans (Kraus, 1995) and then delineate the specific aims and targets of affirmative action policies (Bell, Harrison, & McLaughlin, 2000; Kravitz & Platania, 1993). Fishbein and Ajzen's (1975) theory of reasoned action has often been used as a framework to better understand employees' behavioral support or resistance to affirmative action plans by evaluating employees' attitudes (positive or negative evaluations of affirmative action plans) and subjective norms (the social pressure related to endorsing or not affirmative action plans). For instance, Kravitz and Platania (1993) assessed the beliefs and attitudes toward potential components of affirmative action plans to help reduce conflict related to the implementation of such plans as a function of the target of affirmative action plans (minorities, women, or people with disabilities), which are likely to reveal important differences in Latin American countries with high marks on gender inequity. In the heterogeneous Latin American context, broad categories like native American Indian might not work well in certain countries, where different Indian tribes enjoy a very different socioeconomic status. For example, Otavalo Indians in Ecuador are less marginalized than other Indian ethnicities in Latin America (Riding, 1984). This is in part due to their commercial weaving and related economic success that has not only raised their living standards but also transformed their relationship with whites and mestizos. Therefore, affirmative action programs that benefit Otavalo Indians might be seen with contempt by other minorities in Ecuador.

Future studies may also need to address other questions that can be crucial in the implementation of affirmative action plans in Latin America such as specific measures that could be taken to prevent the stigmatization of affirmative action targets. Should affirmative action programs in Latin America impose fixed employment or admissions quotas like some of those in South Africa and New Zealand? Some argue that such rigid policies have done little to address the educational and work deficiencies of working-class black Africans in South Africa (Herman, 2017), and that they might have actually perpetuated Apartheid principles such as the advancement of certain groups over others for reasons other than merit (Maphai, 1989). Similarly, in New Zealand, quota systems aimed at increasing the number of students from Maori and Pacific Islander ancestry in the field of medicine have been met with controversy (Johnston, 2004).

A series of questions of an economic and national policy nature remains as well. Should the governments of Latin American countries offer fiscal incentives to businesses that put affirmative action programs in place? Should these governments create costly government bureaucracies to monitor the progress of affirmative action programs? Should government contractors be required to have affirmative action plans like those that wish to do business with the US Government? Also, some unique challenges affecting affirmative action plans in Latin America might be related to mastery of the language. For example, for residents of Latin American countries, where the official language is Spanish but whose first language is Quechua or Aymara, should selection tools be modified to prevent adverse impact on them? Should extra credit/points be awarded to those applicants for regional government jobs who are fluent in these languages in the employee selection process like it is done in some autonomous communities in Spain like Catalonia and the Basque country? How should adequate representation of historically marginalized groups among those in charge of recruitment and selection be ensured?

In terms of promoting gender equality, should affirmative action measures in Latin America imitate the German model, whereby a 2001 law imposed gender-based quotas in the hiring of public employees (Stock, 2006)? Or should they adopt an approach similar to Kenya's, where under the 2010 constitution it was established that no single gender should hold more than two-thirds of elected or appointed government positions (Kaimenyi, Kinya, & Macharia Samwel, 2013)? Despite their good intentions, similar policies aimed at achieving gender equality have been met with harsh criticism in New Zealand, whereby a proposal to implement a gender quota system was nicknamed the "man ban" (Whiteacre, 2013; Trevett, 2013). These and many other questions about affirmative action remedies remain to be contextualized and researched in Latin America.

Conclusions

The model described herein provides theoretical insight into the process through which populist-dominated sociopolitical environments might awake already latent attitudes of psychological entitlement among employees in Latin America. We suggest that, if materialized, these attitudes have the potential to ultimately have a negative effect on employees' work performance. The model introduced in this chapter explains the potential process through which these entitlement attitudes emerge and, most importantly, begins to outline solutions like targeted affirmative action programs capable of countering the negative effects of these entitlement attitudes on performance. Further research to contextualize affirmative action plans and related human resource practices to the case of Latin America is warranted to eliminate or at least mitigate the negative spillover effect of political populism to the work sphere of these already vulnerable economies.

References

Ajzen, I. 1985. From intentions to actions: A theory of planned behavior. In J. Kuhl & J. Beckman (Eds.), *Action-control: From cognition to behavior* (pp. 11–39). Heidelberg: Springer.

Ajzen, I. 1987. Attitudes, traits, and actions: Dispositional prediction of behavior in personality and social psychology. In L. Berkowitz (Ed.), *Advances in experimental social psychology* (Vol. 20, pp. 1–63). New York: Academic Press.

Ajzen, I., & Fishbein, M. 1980. *Understanding attitudes and predicting social behavior*. Englewood Cliffs, NJ: Prentice-Hall.

Banco de Santander. 2020. *We're the best bank for diversity and inclusion*. Retrieved from www.santander.com/en/stories/were-the-best-bank-for-diversity-and-inclusion

Bell, M. P., Harrison, D. A., & McLaughlin, M. E. 2000. Forming, changing, and acting on attitude toward affirmative action. *Journal of Applied Psychology*, 85: 784–798.

Bennett-Alexander, D. D. 1990. The state of affirmative action in employment: A post-Stotts retrospective. *American Business Law Journal*, 27: 565–597.

Cachanosky, N., & Padilla, A. 2018. Latin American populism in the Twenty-First Century. *The Independent Review*, 24: 209–226.

Cambridge University Press. 2017, November 30. *The word 'populism' has been announced as the Cambridge Dictionary 2017 Word of the Year*. Retrieved from www.cam.ac.uk/news/populism-revealed-as-2017-word-of-the-year-by-cambridge-university-press

Campbell, W. K., Bonacci, A. M., Shelton, J., Exline, J. J., & Bushman, B. J. 2004. Psychological entitlement: Interpersonal consequences and validation of a self-report measure. *Journal of Personality Assessment*, 83: 29–45.

Cannon, B. 2009. *Hugo Chávez and the Bolivarian revolution: Populism and democracy in a globalized age*. Manchester: Manchester University Press.

Canovan, M. 1999. Trust the people! Populism and the two faces of democracy. *Political Studies*, 47: 2–16.

Cohen-Charash, Y., & Spector, P. E. 2001. The role of justice in organizations: A meta-Analysis. *Organizational Behavior and Human Decision Processes*, 86: 278–321.

Conniff, M. L. 1982. Introduction: Toward a comparative definition of populism. In M. L. Conniff (Ed.), *Latin American populism in comparative perspective* (pp. 3–30). Albuquerque: University of New Mexico Press.

Coronel, G. 2006a, November 27. *Corruption, mismanagement, and abuse of power in Hugo Chávez's Venezuela*. CATO Institute: Center for Global Liberty and Prosperity. Retrieved from www.cato.org/sites/cato.org/files/pubs/pdf/dpa2.pdf

Coronel, G. 2006b, November 30. *Hugo Chávez's unfulfilled promises*. **Cato Institute: Center for Global Liberty and Prosperity**. Retrieved from www.cato.org/publications/commentary/hugo-chavezs-unfulfilled-promises

Crosby, F. J., & VanDeVeer, C. (Eds.). 2000. *Sex, race, and merit: Debating affirmative action in education and employment*. Ann Arbor: University of Michigan Press.

De Dreu, C. K. W., & Weingart, L. R. 2003. Task versus relationship conflict, team performance, and team member satisfaction: A meta-analysis. *Journal of Applied Psychology*, 88: 741–749.

De Ferranti, D., Perry, G. E., Ferreira, F. H. G., & Walton, M. 2004. *Inequality in Latin America: Breaking with history?* World Bank Latin American and Caribbean Studies. Retrieved from https://openknowledge.worldbank.org/handle/10986/15009

de Gaay Fortman, B. 2006. Poverty as a failure of entitlement: Do rights-based approaches make sense? In L. Williams (Ed.), *International poverty law: An emerging discourse* (pp. 34–48). London: Zed Books.

de la Torre, C. 2000. *Populist seduction in Latin America: The Ecuadorian experience*. Athens, OH: Ohio University Center for International Studies.

de la Torre, C. 2015. Introduction: Power to the people? Populism, insurrections, democratization. In C. de la Torre (Ed.), *The promise and perils of populism: Global perspective* (pp. 1–28). Lexington, KE: The University Press of Kentucky.

de la Torre, C. 2017. Populism and nationalism in Latin America. *The Public*, 24: 375–390.

Dobbin, F., Sutton, J. R., Meyer, J. W., & Scott, R. 1993. Equal opportunity law and the construction of internal labor markets. *American Journal of Sociology*, 99: 396–427.

Dornbusch, R., & Edwards, S. 1989. *The macroeconomics of populism in Latin America*. The World Bank: Policy, Planning and Research Department Working Papers. Retrieved from http://documents.worldbank.org/curated/en/823061468776408577/pdf/multi0page.pdf

Ernst, J. 2017, February 27. What is a populist? And is Donald Trump one? *The Atlantic*. Retrieved from www.theatlantic.com/international/archive/2017/02/what-is-populist-trump/516525/

Farh, J. L., & Cheng, B. S. 2000. A cultural analysis of paternalistic leadership in Chinese organizations. In J. T. Li., A. S. Tsui, & E. Weldon (Eds.), *Management and organizations in the Chinese context* (pp. 84–127). London: Palgrave Macmillan.

Fishbein, M., & Ajzen, I. 1975. *Belief, attitude, intention, and behavior*. Reading, MA: Addison-Wesley.

Fishbein, M., & Ajzen, I. 2010. *Predicting and changing behavior: The reasoned action approach*. New York: Routledge.

Garcia, L. T., Erskine, N., Hawn, K., & Casmay, S. R. 1981. The effect of affirmative action on attributions about minority group members. *Journal of Personality*, 49: 427–437.

Gidron, N., & Hall, P. A., 2017. The politics of social status: Economic and cultural roots of the populist right. *The British Journal of Sociology*, 68(S1): S57–S84.

Gomez, C., Kirkman, B. L., & Shapiro, D. L. 2000. The impact of collectivism and in-group/out-group membership on the evaluation generosity of team members. *Academy of management Journal*, 43: 1097–1106.

Gomez, C., & Sanchez, J. I. 2005. HR's strategic role within MNCs: Helping build social capital in Latin America. *The International Journal of International Human Resources Management*, 16: 2189–2200.

Gott, R. 2011. *Hugo Chávez and the Bolivarian Revolution*. Manchester: Manchester University Press.

Harris, M. M., Lievens, F., & Van Hoye, G. 2004. "I think they discriminated against me": Using prototype theory and organizational justice theory for understanding perceived discrimination in selection and promotion situations. *International Journal of Selection and Assessment*, 12(1–2): 54–65.

Harvey, P., & Martinko, M. J. 2008. An empirical examination of the role of attributions in psychological entitlement and its outcomes. *Journal of Organizational Behavior*, 30: 459–476.

Hawkins, K. 2019, August 9. Don't try to silence populists—listen to them. *The Guardian*. Retrieved from www.theguardian.com/world/commentisfree/2019/mar/09/dont-try-to-silence-populists-listen-to-them

Heilman, M. E., Simon, M. C., & Repper, D. P. 1987. Intentionally favored, unintentionally harmed? Impact of sex-based preferential selection on self-perceptions and self-evaluations. *Journal of Applied Psychology*, 72: 62–68.

Herman, H. D. 2017. *Affirmative action in education and Black Economic Empowerment in the workplace in South Africa since 1994: Policies, strengths and limitations*. Bulgaria: Bulgarian Comparative Education Society.

Hoffman, B. J., Blair, C. A., Meriac, J. P., & Woehr, D. J. 2007. Expanding the criterion domain? A quantitative review of the OCB Literature. *Journal of Applied Psychology*, 92: 555–566.

Hofstede, G. H. 1980. *Culture's consequences: International differences in work-related attitudes*. Newbury Park, CA: Sage Publications.

Houle, C., & Kenny, P. D. 2018. The political and economic consequences of populist rule in Latin America. *Government and Opposition*, 53: 256–287.

Inglehart, R. F., & Norris, P. 2016. *Trump, Brexit, and the rise of populism: Economics have-nots and cultural backlash*. Working paper No. RWP16–026, Harvard Kennedy School, Cambridge, MA. Retrieved from https://ssrn.com/abstract=2818659

Johnston, A. 2004. *Students stung by quote backlash*. Retrieved from www.nzherald.co.nz/nz/news/article.cfm?c_id=1&objectid=3552096

Kabeer, N. 1998. Tácticas y compromisos: nexos entre género y pobreza. In I. Arriagada & C. Torres (Eds.), *Género y pobreza. Nuevas dimensiones* (pp. 19–25). Santiago de Chile, Chile: Isis Internacional.

Kaimenyi, C., Kinya, E., & Macharia Samwel, C. 2013. An analysis of affirmative action: The two-thirds gender rule in Kenya. *International Journal of Business, Humanities and Technology*, 3: 91–97.

Kong, W. C. 2014. *Affirmative action or discrimination? A comparative study of higher education in the US and Malaysia*. Selangor, Malaysia: Strategic Information and Research Development Centre.

Kraus, S. J. 1995. Attitudes and the prediction of behavior: A metaanalysis of the empirical literature. *Personality and Social Psychology Bulletin*, 21: 58–74.

Kravitz, D. A. 2008. The diversity-validity dilemma: Beyond selection—the role of affirmative action. *Personnel Psychology*, 61: 173–193.

Kravitz, D. A., Harrison, D. A., Turner, M. E., Levine, E. L., Chaves, W., Brannick, M. T., Denning, D. L., Russell, C. J., & Conard, M. A. 1997. *Affirmative action: A review of psychological and behavioral research*. Bowling Green, OH: Society for Industrial and Organizational Psychology.

Kravitz, D. A., & Platania, J. 1993. Attitudes and beliefs about affirmative action: Effects of target and of respondent sex and ethnicity. *Journal of Applied Psychology*, 78: 928–938.

Kurmanaev, A. 2020, July 29. Latin America is facing a decline of democracy under the pandemic. *The New York Times*. Retrieved from www.nytimes.com/2020/07/29/world/americas/latin-america-democracy-pandemic.html

Laclau, E. 1977. *Politics and ideology in Marxist theory*. London: Verso.

La Nación. 2007, March 30. *Problemas para la principal fuente de ingresos de Hugo Chávez. El gasto social golpea las arcas de Pdvsa: Las ganancias de la petrolera venezolana se redujeron por el fuerte aumento en los programas sociales*. Retrieved from www.lanacion.com.ar/el-mundo/el-gasto-social-golpea-las-arcas-de-pdvsa-nid895719/

Laurence, M. 2016. The triumph of politics: The return of the left in Venezuela, Bolivia and Ecuador. *The European Legacy*, 21: 103–105.

Leslie, L. M., Mayer, D. M., & Kravitz, D. A. 2014. The stigma of affirmative action: A stereotyping-based theory and meta-analytic test of the consequences for performance. *Academy of Management*, 57: 964–989.

MacKenzie, S. B., Posakoff, P. M., & Fetter, R. 1991. Organizational citizenship behavior and objective productivity as determinants of managerial evaluations of salesperson's performance. *Organizational Behavior and Human Decision Processes*, 50: 123–150.

Madrid, R. L., Hunter, W., & Weyland, K. 2010. The policies and performance of the contestatory and moderate left. In K. Weyland, R. Madrid, & W. Hunterd (Eds.), *Leftist governments in Latin America: Success and Shortcomings* (pp. 140–180). New York: Cambridge University Press.

Maphai, V. T. 1989. Affirmative action in South Africa—a genuine option? *Social Dynamics*, 15: 1–24.

Martinez, P. G. 2005. Paternalism as a positive form of leadership in the Latin American context: Leader benevolence, decision-making control and human resource management practices. In M. Elvira & A. Davilla (Eds.), *Managing human resources in Latin America: An agenda for international leaders* (pp. 75–93). New York: Routledge.

Moffitt, B. 2017. *The global rise of populism: Performance, political style and representation. Redwood*. Redwood City, CA: Stanford University Press.

Moffitt, B., & Tormey, S. 2014. Rethinking populism: Politics, mediatisation and political style. *Political Studies*, 62: 381–397.

Morgan, J. 2019, November 22. Capital flight takes off in Venezuela. *Latin American Herald Tribune*. Retrieved from www.laht.com/article.asp?ArticleId=32060 7&CategoryId=10717

Mudde, C. 2004. The populist Zeitgeist. *Government and Opposition*, 39: 541–563.

Mudde, C., & Kaltwasser, C. R. 2013. Exclusionary vs. inclusionary populism: Comparing contemporary Europe and Latin America. *Government and Opposition*, 48: 147–174.

Muhr, T., & Verger, A. 2006. Venezuela: Higher education for all. *Journal of Critical Education Policy Studies*, 4: 160–194.

Mullingan, T. 2020. *Quotas are still impermissible in terms of the Employment Equity Act*. The South African Labor Guide: Your Guide to Labour Law in South Africa. Retrieved from www.labourguide.co.za/most-recent/2265-quotas-are-still-impermissible-in-terms-of-the-employment-equity-act

Niemann, Y. F., & Dovidio, J. F. 2005. Affirmative action and job satisfaction: Understanding underlying processes. *Journal of Social Issues*, 61: 507–523.

Organ, D. W. 1988. *Organizational citizenship behavior: The good soldier syndrome*. Lexington, MA: Lexington Books.

Oxendine, A. R. 2019. The political psychology of inequality and why it matters for populism. *International Perspectives in Psychology: Research, Practice, Consultation*, 8: 179–195.

Panizza, F. 2009. *Contemporary Latin America: Development and democracy beyond the Washington consensus*. New York, Zed Books.

Pettigrew, T. F., & Martin, J. 1987. Shaping the organizational context for Black American inclusion. *Journal of Social Issues*, 43: 41–78.

Preissler Iglesia, S., Viotti Beck, M., & Adghirni, S. 2020, April 26. Bolsonaro bet big with two promises and both are in trouble. *Bloomberg*. Retrieved from www.bloomberg.com/news/articles/2020-04-25/bolsonaro-bet-big-with-two-promises-and-both-are-faltering

Rahim, M. A., Antonioni, D., Krumov, K., & Ilieva, S. 2000. Power, conflict, and effectiveness: A cross-cultural study in the United States and Bulgaria. *European Psychologist*, 5: 28–33.

Riding, A. 1984, May 15. For Ecuador Indians, pride and profits in weaving. *The New York Times*. Retrieved from www.nytimes.com/1984/05/15/world/for-ecuador-indians-pride-and-profits-in-weaving.html

Rodríguez Braun, C. 2012. The values of free enterprise versus the new populism in Latin America. *The Independent Review*, 17: 19–34.

Sánchez, V. 2019, August. Venezuela hyperinflation hits 10 million percent: 'Shock therapy' may be only chance to undo the economic damage. *CNBC News*. Retrieved from www.cnbc.com/2019/08/02/venezuela-inflation-at-10-million-percent-its-time-for-shock-therapy.html

Selçuk, O. 2016. Strong presidents and weak institutions: Populism in Turkey, Venezuela and Ecuador. *Southeast European and Black Sea Studies*, 16: 571–589.

Stavrakakis, Y., & Katsambekis, G. 2014. Left-wing populism in the European periphery: The case of Syriza. *Journal of Political Ideologies*, 19: 119–142.

Stavrakakis, Y., Kioupkiolis, A., Katsambekis, G., Nikisianis, N., & Siomos, T. 2016. Contemporary left-wing populism in Latin America: Leadership, horizontalism, and postdemocracy. *Latin American Politics and Society*, 58: 51–76.

Stiglitz, J., 2003, July 7. Populists are sometimes right. *Project Syndicate: The World's Opinion Page*. Retrieved from www.project-syndicate.org/commentary/populists-are-sometimes-right?barrier=accesspaylog

Stock, A. J. 2006. Affirmative action: A German perspective on the promotion of women's rights with regard to employment. *Journal of Law and Society*, 33: 59–73.

Stromquist, N. P. 2004. Inequality as a way of life: Education and social class in Latin America. *Pedagogy, Culture and Society*, 12: 95–119.

Tajfel, H. 1974. Social identity and intergroup behavior. *Social Science Information*, 13: 65–93.

Takeuchi, R., Wang, A. C., & Farh, J. L. 2020. Asian conceptualizations of leadership: Progresses and challenges. *Annual Review of Organizational Psychology and Organizational Behavior*, 7: 233–256.

Tian, Q., & Sanchez, J. I. 2017. Does paternalistic leadership promote innovative behavior? The interaction between authoritarianism and benevolence. *Journal of Applied Social Psychology*, 47: 235–246.

Tiwari, M. 2007. Chronic poverty and entitlement theory. *Third World Quarterly*, 28: 171–191.

Trevett, C. 2013. *Labour backs away from man-ban plan*. Retrieved from www.nzherald.co.nz/nz/news/article.cfm?c_id= 1&objectid=10895712

Wated, G., Sanchez, J. I., & Gomez, C. 2008. Two-factor assessment of the beliefs that influence attitudes toward privatization. *Group and Organization Management*, 33: 107–136.

Wejnert, B. 2014. Epilogue: Finding populism today. In D. Woods & B. Wejnert (Eds.), *The many faces of populism: Current perspectives* (pp. 163–172). Bingley, UK: Emerald Group Publishing Limited.

Whiteacre, C. 2013. *Labour pushes for 'man ban'*. Retrieved from www.3news.co.nz/politics/labour-party-pushes-for-man-ban2013070416#axzz3bgqrmJ9X

Whitman, D. S., Caleo, S., Carpenter, N. C., Horner, M. T., & Bernerth, J. B. 2012. Fairness at the collective level: A meta-analytic examination of the consequences and boundary conditions of organizational justice climate. *Journal of Applied Psychology*, 97: 776–791.

Woods, D. 2014. The many faces of populism: Diverse but not disparate. In D. Woods & B. Wejnert (Eds.), *The many faces of populism: Current perspectives* (pp. 1–25). Bingley, UK: Emerald Group Publishing Limited.

3 The Emergence of the Self-Employed Worker in Brazil

Toward a Structural Change of the Labor Market

Wilson Aparecido Costa de Amorim,
Antonio Carvalho Neto and
Lúcia Dos Santos Garcia

Introduction

During the 1990s, the successful economic stabilization in Brazil, together with a significant drop of the inflation rate happened in a scenario of high interest rates and exposure to international competition. In the labor market, there was a rise in unemployment and a drop in income until the early 2000s (Dedecca, 2005).

From 2003 to 2014 there was sufficient economic growth, which resulted in a significant drop in unemployment. Some of the main metropolitan regions of Brazil, such as Porto Alegre and Belo Horizonte reached levels close to full employment (Amorim, 2015; Menezes Filho, Cabanas & Komatsu, 2014).

The profiles of labor supply and demand in the main metropolitan regions of Brazil have changed a lot from the 1990s to 2020. The number of older workers among those employed grew (26% of workers aged 50 years or more in 2015 versus 17% in 2003). The increase in the participation of the highest levels of schooling was substantial (66% have 11 or more years of study in 2015 versus 46.7% in 2003). The number of women also increased (46% in 2015 versus 43% in 2003) (IBGE, 2016a).

From 2015 until 2019 the deep economic recession in Brazil raised the unemployment rate and brought down the workers' income, eliminating around two million formal jobs in the private sector (CAGED, July 2019), which corresponds to a 3.5% decrease in the number of employees.

However, the economic crisis is not the only factor redesigning the Brazilian labor market. At least three other factors need to be taken into account: the Labor Reform, the liberal political profile of the Bolsonaro government and the Revolution 4.0. These three factors are intertwined with the economic crisis and result in the emergence of self-employed workers[1] as one of the main segments of the informal sector, the object of study in this chapter.

Allied to these factors, the economic crisis of unimaginable dimensions caused by the coronavirus pandemic was worsened by the Brazilian government's denial of its seriousness. The recovery of the Brazilian economy was delayed and consequently the unemployment rate was the highest since 2012 (13.3% in June 2020). Based on this scenario, Brazil seems to be moving toward a labor market structured in at least three segments.

At the top is the segment composed by workers whose families earn a "high" or "upper middle" average income (something like 4.7% of the households according to *IBGE—PNAD*). This segment has better paid jobs, more stable and formal employment contracts and better quality jobs.

The second segment (around 80% of the households) is composed by workers whose families earn, in average, from middle to low income. In this segment, the more flexible and wage-reducing labor legislation worsens the conditions for individual and collective bargains. The third segment (around 15.3% of the households) is composed by workers whose families do not earn any income.

Between the second and the third segments there is a group of workers whose number range from 20 million to 28.5 million people, who, according to the *IBGE—PNAD* (August 2019), are either unemployed, under-employed, or considered potential workforce.[2] The flexibilization of the legislation brought by the Labor Reform made hiring and firing procedures less costly and less procedurally complicated (Adascalitei & Pigntatti Morano, 2015). In this context and without economic growth more workers will be squeezed between these two segments.

This chapter will analyze the profile of this group of workers, with special attention to those who have become individual micro entrepreneurs, but who are in the informal sector, and those who are under-employed (that is, they could find only part time jobs and flexiwork, gigs). This group is already been affected by the four factors acting upon the Brazilian labor market: a strong economic recession, the accelerated introduction of information technologies and digital business platforms, the recent Labor Reform, and an ultraliberal government that has been rapidly dismantling previous social protection structures.

In this chapter, we will address these four interconnected factors, which are responsible for the significant increase in the amount of self-employed workers, before we go into a more detailed analysis of who these workers are. Our findings also hold significant implications for companies that already operate or intend to operate in Brazil.

Four Key Factors Responsible for the Structural Change in the Brazilian Labor Market

The Brazilian labor market is structurally heterogeneous and unequal. This heterogeneity has been even more pronounced due to four interdependent phenomena whose interaction intensified greatly after 2014: the ongoing technological transition; the labor reform; the effects of the economic crisis on the labor market; and from 2019 onwards the liberal profile of the Bolsonaro government.

The Technological Transition: Industry 4.0, Digital Platforms, and the Gig Economy

An international phenomenon, industry 4.0, is an important factor also affecting the Brazilian labor market. The increasing speed with which information technology and digitalization has been reshaping production processes and the very nature of work is rather impressive (Findlay & Thompson, 2017; Wright, Wailes, Bamber, & Lansbury, 2017).

Due to its structural character, this factor conditions the other three that are also responsible for the structural change in the Brazilian labor market. There is an accelerated elimination of both unskilled and skilled jobs in the whole economy (Kurt, 2019; Dean & Spoehr, 2018) even in countries much more developed than Brazil such as Japan (Riminucci, 2018) and the US (Frey & Osborne, 2017). The industry 4.0 is reshaping small businesses and big companies due to the automation and streamlining in the use of information combined with artificial intelligence, data mining, and e-business based on digital platforms.

This industry 4.0 is at odds with regulation due to its decentralized nature from the point of view of the customers and workers. There is clearly greater insecurity regarding employment (Findlay & Thompson, 2017), brought on by the flexibilization of contracts and by the exponential increase in production on demand. One of the most visible examples is the so-called work "uberization," the flexibilization of social protection that brought flexible working hours, informal contracts and compensation (Codagnone & Martens, 2016). Indeed, an elastic supply of drivers, motorcyclists, cyclists, and deliverers of e-commerce goods (Graham, Hjorth, & Lehdonvirta, 2017) has joined the already pre-existing enormous army of Brazilian informal workers. This army of "uberized" workers carried out an unprecedented one-day strike on July 1, 2020 in several large Brazilian cities demanding higher compensation, health insurance, food aid grant, and hygiene kits to prevent coronavirus contagion. These motorcyclists and cyclists, most of them young people, are around four million, not included uber drivers.

There was also an irreversible penetration of these digital platforms in business in the areas of tourism, real estate, insurance, and finance. Here, technology 4.0 seeks and sponsors flexibilization in hiring.

Deregulation of Work: The Labor Legislation Reform of November 2017

The labor reform that came into force in November 2017 was driven by the government of President Temer, with the support of the employers' national associations and their representatives in Congress, as well as the higher Labor Court. There was no discussion with trade unions. The Reform took only seven months from beginning to end, and resulted in the most radical cut in employee rights in 70 years.

The reform suppressed, modified, and included 111 laws. We describe here some of the most dramatic, so to speak. The Reform enabled a direct agreement between employer and employee at the individual level to reduce wages, some rights, and benefits. Before the reform there was neither any individual agreement nor any possibility of reducing wages; reducing rights and benefits was extremely difficult before the reform. In addition, the reform facilitated a much more flexible employment contract (flexible working schedules) without union protection. The reform introduced the possibility of massive layoffs, without any discussion with trade unions. It is not mandatory any more for the employer to terminate the individual contract with the union inspection. The decentralized collective bargaining at firm level gained preponderance over the centralized collective bargaining at the economic sectorial level, which weakened the bargaining power of trade unions. The reform also restricted workers' free access to the Labor Court, which existed until then (Krein, 2018).

Before the Reform, the Brazilian Labor Relations System could historically be classified as hybrid, as it was regulated for about half of the labor force with a formal employment contract and virtually deregulated for the other half, informal workers (Carvalho Neto, Amorim, & Fischer, 2016), who never had any labor rights. After the 2017 reform, the Brazilian System moved closer to the US voluntary labor relations system. Brazilian labor reform, even brusque and radical, is part of the international movement to enhance greater work deregulation of work that has been taking place gradually for at least three decades in successive waves (Carvalho Neto et al., 2016). This movement has deepened the deregulation in countries that have Labor Relations Systems with a voluntary or liberal tradition like the US and the United Kingdom or decreasing the degree of regulation in countries that have systems with a regulated or coordinated tradition such as Germany, France, and Sweden (Hyman, 2018; Hall & Soskice, 2003).

Regarding the effects of the labor reform on the Brazilian labor market, given the low dynamism of the economy, it is still not possible to say that the more flexible forms of labor contracting have spread across the various economic sectors. With the economy growing little, there are few new job offers. Thus, part-time, intermittent, and other flexible work modalities, introduced and expanded by labor reform, are still not very significant in the official statistics to enable consistent conclusions in 2018 and 2019 (MTE— CAGED, 2019). On the other hand, Labor Courts' statistics clearly show a huge drop in the lawsuits filed by workers against employers in Brazil, as a result of the restrictions imposed by the reform on the workers' free access to the Labor Courts.

The Brazilian Liberal Government

Another factor that contributes to the worsening of the labor market situation is the position of the Bolsonaro government, openly in favor of minimal labor protection. The government has dismantled the state's inspection apparatus enforcing workers' rights protection. A clear example in this direction was the abolishment of the Ministry of Labor (ending a 90-year history), with the creation of a department with reduced functions under the Ministry of the Economy in its place. The liberal government has no affinity with active policies to generate employment, jobs and income (Amorim, 2020). On the contrary, the government announced its intention to enforce an even more radical deregulation of labor legislation than the one that took place with the Labor Reform, with the introduction of a new contract, where the workers' rights are significantly reduced.

The government has led the public debate based on an exclusive binary logic in which "the worker has the choice between having more rights and no job or a job and no rights" (Filgueiras, 2019). There was a social security reform during Bolsonaro's government at the end of 2019 that also favors cheaper labor contracts by defining a longer working time requirement for the worker to retire (DIEESE, 2019).

Brazilian Labor Market and the Economic Crisis

Regarding this section, for a better understanding of the data on the Brazilian labor market, we initially present the main characteristics of the Continuous PNAD—Continuous National Household Sample Survey—which is carried out by IBGE—Brazilian Institute of Geography and Statistics. Then, we describe and analyze data on the effects of the economic crisis on the labor market.

Table 3.1 PNAD Contínua—Main Features

Features	Description
Periodicity of results disclosure	Monthly, quarterly, annual
Coverage	National (3,500 cities), around 210,000 households (visited each quarterly)
Survey Unit	Household
Tool of research	Questionnaire answered during an interview (32 pages)
Indicators	The workforce (quarterly) and annual indicators on permanent supplementary themes (such as employment and other forms of work, personal and household care, information and communication technology, etc.)

Source: IBGE (2014)

Measuring the Brazilian labor market—PNAD/IBGE. IBGE is the main producer of statistics of economic, social, and demographic nature in Brazil. Since the early 1980s, IBGE has been conducting regular surveys on the labor market. The Continuous PNAD is a sample survey that has been carried out since 2012.

The survey is nationwide and regularly discloses various economic and social indicators. With regard to the labor market, PNAD Continua is in line with ILO guidelines and seeks to identify in more detail aspects related to informality and/or precariousness of forms of occupation (IBGE, 2014).

Given the great heterogeneity of the Brazilian labor market, it is possible to identify occupations among salaried workers in companies in the private sector, in the public sector, in household services, among self-employed workers, in addition to groups of auxiliary family workers. The survey also considers information related to employers, that is, business owners who have employees.

Within the Brazilian labor market it is possible to observe aspects of underdeveloped economies such as the large presence of workers in household services and even auxiliary family workers. The survey allows to identify and estimate the number of informal workers and formal workers in precarious working conditions in all these types of occupation.

The effects of the economic crisis in the Brazilian labor markets. The deep downturn in economic activity that took place in Brazil after 2014 caused an increase in the unemployment rate in the labor market, as seen in Table 3.2.

Table 3.2 Brazilian Labor Market—Selected Indicators (annual averages) (thousands)

Indicators	2014	2015	2016	2017	2018	2019
Employed population	91,638	91,685	89,975	90,294	91,571	93,390
Unemployed	6,699	8,531	11,696	13,176	12,790	12,575
Unemployment Rate (%)	6.8	8.5	11.5	12.9	12.3	11.9

Source: PNAD Contínua, IBGE—2012–2019. Elaborated by the authors.

Between 2014 and 2019, the unemployed workers went from 6.7 million to 12.6 million in Brazil. Along with this increase in unemployment, there was a huge growth in informal work.

According to Table 3.3, which is presented in the next section, more than 12 million informal workers can be found in the private sector in 2019, that is, almost 1.4 million more informal workers than in 2014. Regarding the magnitude of these numbers, it is important to remember that if there are informal wage earners it is because there are companies that hire them with no formal contract. These contracting arrangements, which became part of the Brazilian labor scenario since long ago, occur outside the labor legislation. It is a historical "no rights land", the same one that the Bolsonaro government intended to legalize.

Since the beginning of the Brazilian economic recession in late 2014, the number of employees holding a formal contract in the private sector has shrunk by around two million jobs. During the same period, the precarious contracts in the private sector, that is, without any signed record, showed growth around 1.4 million, as we can see in Table 3.3 next section.

The Emergence of the Self-Employed Worker

Since they are at the base of the Brazilian social pyramid in their vast majority, self-employed workers are the group that has suffered the most from the combined impacts of the economic crisis, the labor reform, the new configuration of work brought about by the digital platforms, and the radical flexibility promoted by the government. These workers have neither the defense mechanisms of the most qualified workers nor the social networks capable of directing them to better job opportunities. This is aggravated in a profoundly unequal society like the Brazilian one.

Table 3.3 presents occupied people (considered as those workers and employers who are either in the formal or in the informal market together)

Table 3.3 Estimated number of employed persons, according to forms of inclusion, Brazil—2012–2019

Forms of Inclusion	Periods (thousands)			Relative Variations (%)		
	2012	2014	2019	2019 / 2012	2014 / 2012	2019 / 2014
Total Employment	89,234	91,945	94,641	6.1	3.0	2.9
Employees	62,548	64,221	63,771	2.0	2.7	−0.7
Formal hiring in	*44,925*	*47,260*	*44,804*	0.3	5.2	5.2
Private companies	34,253	36,149	33,909	−1.0	5.5	6.2
Public sector	8,786	9,197	9,169	4.4	4.7	−0.3
Households services	1,886	1,914	1,726	−8.5	1.5	−9.8
Informal hiring in	*17,623*	*16,961*	*18,967*	7.6	−3.8	11.8
Private companies	11,126	10,619	12,009	7.9	−4.6	13.1
Public sector	2,194	2,259	2,472	12.7	3.0	9.4
Households services	4,303	4,083	4,486	4.3	−5.1	9.9
Employers	3,541	3,811	4,370	23.4	7.6	14.7
Self-employed	20,387	21,291	24,416	19.8	4.4	14.7
Auxiliary family worker	2,758	2,622	2,084	−24.4	−4.9	−20.5

Source: PNAD Contínua, IBGE. Elaborated by the authors.

according to the PNAD Contínua. We show below some general findings about the 2019 data. The first finding is that the demand side (contracting by companies and governments) in the Brazilian labor market is very diversified in its hiring forms. These occupied people may be self-employed workers such as psychologists, consultants, lawyers and, in much greater proportion, plumbers, masons, electricians, joiners, computer technicians, manicurists, hairdressers, and street vendors. They can be also employers, from the micro-entrepreneur to the owner of a large company, as long as he hires at least one employee. They can also be employees with formal employment contract in the public and private sectors. Furthermore, they may be working in households (cleaners, cooks, babysitters, laundresses). Finally, they can be auxiliary family workers (children and relatives working in the family business without pay).

A second finding about 2019 data shown in Table 3.3 is that this diversity of forms of hiring occurs with a high participation of jobs without any formal employment contract or protected by the country's legislation. Among the workers employed by the private sector, almost a third (26.2%) did not have formal contracts. This proportion was even higher among household workers, since approximately three out of four are also in this same condition. In the set of all forms of hiring by companies, governments, and households together, which otaled 63,771 thousand employees, 18,967, (29.7%) maintained informal arrangements with their employers.

A third finding about 2019 data shown in Table 3.3 is that the number of employees raised just a little from 2012 to 2019 (only 2.0%), while the occupied people in general increased by 6.1%. This difference shows that there is some kind of inclusion in the Brazilian labor market in addition to wage earning. The answer can be found in self-employed workers. From 2012 to 2019, this group of workers reached 24.4 million, a rather significant growth of 19.8% in the period. Thus, one in four of occupied individuals in Brazil already works using his or her own resources, as an entrepreneur of himself or herself.

An important structural change is thus taking place in the Brazilian labor market, which goes beyond cyclical fluctuations in production and employment. The basic characteristic of this change is the loss of traditional salaried jobs with formal contracts in private companies, coupled with an increase in self-employment. Figure 3.1 below reveals how this structural change occurred in the period we studied.

Figure 3.1 shows the behavior of the occupied people over the period studied. The employer and self-employed groups had the most significant

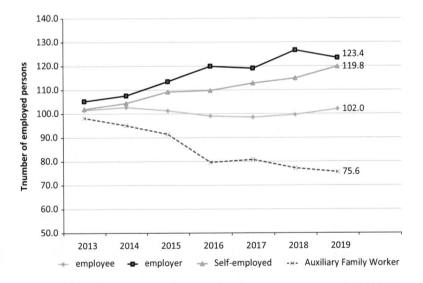

Figure 3.1 Evolution rate of groupings of employed persons in Brazil—2012 to 2019 (2012 = 100)

Source: PNAD Contínua, IBGE.

(Note: The "Employee" grouping contains private and public sector employees)

variations in their amount. Among employers, there was an increase of 23.4% over the entire period. Among self-employed workers, the variation was almost 20%. The structural change of the Brazilian labor market takes shape through self-employed workers, since the growth in its group is much more significant than in the other segments: 24.4 million people in 2019 against 20 million in 2012, as we can see in Figure 3.1.

These self-employed workers deal mainly in service provision and, in this condition, are very dependent on the pace of the economic activity in the country, as the ones who hire them are families and companies, closely linked to the economy's disposable income. In times of crisis, families and companies spend less money, and hire less. Thus, this study contributes to a greater knowledge about these self-employed workers whose expressive increase is a fact worth noting in Brazil.

In Table 3.4 it can be seen that, among people who are self-employed, around 24.4 million work without a *CNPJ*[3] registration, that is, informally, without any contract. This number corresponds to 79.9% of the total. The remaining 4.9 million maintain work with the formal *CNPJ* registration. The respective data is in Table 3.4.

Table 3.5 shows that self-employed workers are in their largest proportion in the services sector (39.7%), both gross and retail (20.5%). Less

Table 3.4 Self-employed workers—Distribution by Formality of Activity Brazil—2019 (%)

Data	Total	Formal	Informal
Number—(thousands)	24,416 4.917 19.499	4,917 19.499	19,499
Participation	100.0	20.1	79.9

Source: PNAD Contínua, IBGE. Elaborated by the authors.

Table 3.5 Self-employed workers—Distribution by Economic Sector—Brazil—2019 (%)

Sector	Total	Formal	Informal
Agriculture, etc.*	15.0	5.4	17.5
General industry	10.1	9.0	10.3
Construction	14.6	7.2	16.5
Gross and Retail	20.5	29.0	18.3
Services	39.7	49.4	37.3
Total	100.0	100.0	100.0

* Agriculture, livestock, forest production, fisheries, and aquaculture.
Source: PNAD Contínua, IBGE. Elaborated by the authors.

frequently, self-employment market entry is in production activities—agriculture and livestock, industry and construction. Within the services sector, practically half of the formal jobs are self-employment, followed by gross and retail, with 29.0%. The other economic sectors have a very small share of formally employed persons. Among the informal self-employment jobs, the largest proportion is again in the services sector, with 37.3% of the total.

Table 3.6 shows the profile of self-employed workers according to personal characteristics. From the gender point of view, self-employed workers are predominantly men, in a proportion of approximately two men for each woman in this condition. This proportion is relatively similar when observing the distribution of gender in formally registered business and informal insertions.

The age group with the highest participation is between 36 and 49 years old (33.7%). There is also a high participation among older workers, since

Table 3.6 Self-employed workers—Distribution by personal characteristics—Brazil—2019 (%)

Characteristics	Total	Formal	Informal
Sex			
Man	64.7	61.8	65.5
Woman	35.3	38.2	34.5
Total	100.0	100.0	100.0
Age	**Total**	**Formal**	**Informal**
From 14 to 24 years	8.1	4.9	8.9
From 25 to 35 years	22.5	24.2	22.0
From 36 to 49 years	33.7	38.4	32.5
From 50 to 59 years	21.9	21.3	22.0
60 years or more	13.9	11.2	14.6
Total	100.0	100.0	100.0
Education level	**Total**	**Formal**	**Informal**
Uneducated and incomplete elementary school	36.8	18.2	41.5
Complete elementary school and incomplete high school	16.7	13.3	17.6
Complete high school and incomplete college education	33.4	41.2	31.4
College degree	13.1	27.3	9.6
Total	100.0	100.0	100.0
Mean usual real income Value (in 2019 R$)	**Total** 1,660	**Formal** 2,944	**Informal** 1,337

Source: PNAD Contínua, IBGE. Elaborated by the authors.

Table 3.7 Self-employed workers—Distribution by Individual Contribution to Social Security—Brazil—2019 (%)

Individual Contribution	Total	Formal	Informal
Contributes	29.8	72.7	19.0
Does not contribute	70.2	27.3	81.0
Total	100.0	100.0	100.0

Source: PNAD Contínua, IBGE. Elaborated by the authors.

about 36% of the total corresponds to the group of employed persons aged 50 or over. Such proportions are relatively similar when looking at self-employed workers according to the formality of their contract.

In another relevant aspect it is noted that, for the general total of self-employed workers, the highest proportion is of workers with a lower education level (without education and incomplete elementary school), 36.8%. When we observe informally self-employed workers separately, this proportion is even higher (41.5%). On the other hand, among formally self-employed workers, there is a higher proportion of workers with a higher education level: 41.2% with complete high school and incomplete college education and 27.3% with a college degree.

As for their level of income, self-employed workers present very different values depending on their formality situation. Self-employed workers with formal business registration earn R$ 2,944 (approximately US$ 730 in December 2019) while informal workers under this condition earn less than half of that, R$ 1,337 (approximately US$ 330 in December 2019). Such values indicate that among self-employed workers, who perform activities with lower compensation, there is certainly greater difficulty in meeting the requirements and costs posed to maintain the economic activity, such as legal registration and tax collection.

Table 3.7 shows that the vast majority of self-employed workers in Brazil (70.2%) do not contribute individually to Social Security. The general proportion of non-contributors to Social Security is related to the group of informally self-employed workers. In this group, only 19.0% contribute individually to Social Security. Among formally self-employed workers, the picture is the opposite, since 72.7% of them contribute.

Final Considerations

The data presented in this chapter reveal that there has been a structural change in the Brazilian labor market in the last few years, due to the growing participation of self-employed workers, together with a drop in employees with formal wage contracts.

This structural change in the Brazilian labor market seems to reveal two clearly distinctive groups and a significant segmentation of the labor market. One group is composed by employees with formal wage contracts (around 40 million workers in 2019), and another one is formed by those self-employed (around 24.4 million in 2019). In the first group, we find highly educated individuals, with better levels of compensation and a higher "degree of citizenship", given their higher contribution to Social Security. The second group, instead, includes self-employed workers, from which 80% are informal, have less education, earn a lower income, and often do not contribute to Social Security. This second group is also significantly concentrated in the service sector, which reflects the sector's own increasing participation within the economy as a whole. Our findings show that there is a clear need to study this new form of labor market entry, opening up research and public policy agendas in Brazil and everywhere.

According to economic crisis-fighting manuals, there is consensus among economists from the most diverse lines of thought, except for those who belong to the liberal group that composes or supports the current Brazilian government, that without an anti-cyclical economic policy there is no quick way out of recession (Pastore, 2020; Luque, Silber, Luna, & Zagha, 2020; IMF, 2020). These policies would foster employment in strategic sectors aiming long-term sustainability in sufficient time and volume to bring back the investor confidence. Such policies, associated with other active and passive policies in the labor market (those aimed at occupational training for example) could lessen the worker's distress, especially in the segment highlighted in this chapter (OIT, 2020).

For companies that already operate or intend to operate in Brazil, the expansion of the self-employed participation in the labor market also has important implications. As self-employed contractors, firms need to hire carefully following the existent legislation, avoiding informal agreements. The Brazilian government, due to the expansion of self-employment, took steps toward formalizing their hiring by companies, such as, for example, forcing firms to a mandatory social security payment (Ansiliero & Constanzi, 2017) or establishing penalties for those who want to transform *de facto* formal employee relationships into self-employed schemes.

Another implication from the growth of the self-employed, in line with the previous, is that firms operating in Brazil will increasingly need to train and develop self-employed contract managers, who are well aware of the new legislation, and avoid tax or social security liabilities. These managers will need to work in collaboration with other line managers, who are often the ones demanding self-employed contracts.

Last but not least, foreign multinationals operating in Brazil need to be aware of the high proportion of informal self-employed in the Brazilian labor market, and take the necessary steps to make sure that their hiring is in line with the standards that respect workers' rights. Both ethically and reputationally, being proactive in dealing with the self-employed will increase these firms' ability to attract the best talent in the region.

Notes

1. "Self-employed" is a person who works using his/her own enterprise, alone or with a partner, without having employees, and with or without relying on the help of an unpaid worker from a member of the same household where they reside. "Employer" is the person who works using his/her own enterprise, having at least one employee, and with or without relying on the help of an unpaid worker from a member of the same household (IBGE, 2019).
2. The potential workforce is measured by the Brazilian Institute of Geography and Statistics (IBGE) and is defined as "the group of people (age 14 and over) who were neither employed nor unemployed during the week that was researched, but who had a potential to transform into workforce. This contingent is composed by two groups: I. people who did an effective job search, but were not able to find a job; II. people who did not carry out an effective job search but would like to have a job and were available to work" (IBGE, 2016b).
3. In Brazil, the National Register of Legal Entities (*CNPJ*) provides a unique number that identifies a legal entity, i.e., a company or other kind of legal arrangement with the Federal Revenue Service.

References

Adascalitei, D., & Pignatti Morano, C. 2015. *Labour market reforms since the crisis: Drivers and consequences.* International Labour Office, Research Department. Geneva: ILO, Research Department Working Paper; No. 5.

Amorim, W. A. C. 2015. *Negociações Coletivas no Brasil: 50 anos de aprendizado.* São Paulo: Atlas.

Amorim, W. A. C. 2020. September–October. The future of work in Brazil: Looking after institutions. *RAE*, 60(5): 371–377. São Paulo.

Ansiliero, G., & Costanzi, R. N. 2017. *Cobertura e padrão de inserção previdenciária dos trabalhadores autônomos no regime geral de previdência social.* Instituto de Pesquisa Econômica Aplicada. Brasília: Rio de Janeiro: Ipea, Texto para discussão n° 2342.

Carvalho Neto, A., Amorim, W. A. C., & Fischer, A. L. 2016. Top human resources managers views on trade union action in Brazilian corporations. Brazilian *Administration* Review, 13(4): 1–23.

Codagnone, C., & Martens, B. 2016. *Scoping the sharing economy: Origins, definitions, impact and regulatory issues.* Institute for Prospective Technological Studies Digital Economy Working Paper 2016/01. JRC100369.

Dean, M., & Spoehr, J. 2018. The fourth industrial revolution and the future of manufacturing work in Australia: Challenges and opportunities. *Labor & Industry: A Journal of the Social and Economic Relations of Work*, 28(3): 166–181.

Dedecca, C. S. 2005, janeiro–março. Notas sobre a evolução do mercado de trabalho brasileiro. *Revista de Economia Política*, 25(1): 94–111.

DIEESE—Departamento Intersindical de Estatística e Estudos Socioeconômicos. 2019, Novembro. PEC 6/2019: como ficou a Previdência depois da aprovação da reforma no Senado Federal. *Nota Técnica* Número 214.

Filgueiras, V. A. 2019. As promessas da Reforma Trabalhista: combate ao desemprego e redução da informalidade. In J. D. Krein, R. O. Véras, & V. A. Filgueiras (orgs.), *Reforma trabalhista no Brasil: promessas e realidade/*Organizadores. Campinas, SP: Curt Nimuendajú, 222 p.

Findlay, P., & Thompson, P. 2017. Contemporary work: Its meanings and demands. Journal of Industrial Relations, 59(2): 122–138.

Frey, C. B., & Osborne, M. A. 2017. The future of employment: How susceptible are jobs to computerisation? *Technological Forecasting and Social Change*, 114: 254–280.

Graham, M., Hjorth, I., & Lehdonvirta, V. 2017. Digital labor and development: Impacts of global digital labor platforms and the gig economy on worker livelihoods. *European Review of Labor and Research*, 23(2): 135–162.

Hall, P., & Soskice, D. (Eds.). 2003. *Varieties of capitalism—The institutional foundations of comparative advantage*. Oxford: Oxford University Press.

Hyman, R. 2018. What future for industrial relations in Europe? *Employee Relations*, 40(4): 569–579.

IBGE – Instituto Brasileiro de Geografia e Estatística. 2014. *Notas Metodológicas – Volume 1*. Rio de Janeiro: IBGE.

IBGE – Instituto Brasileiro de Geografia e Estatística. 2016a. *Pesquisa Mensal de Emprego*. Indicadores IBGE. Principais destaques da evolução do mercado de trabalho nas regiões metropolitanas abrangidas pela pesquisa 2003-2015. Rio de Janeiro: IBGE.

IBGE—Instituto Brasileiro de Geografia e Estatística. 2016b. *Pesquisa Mensal de Emprego*. Indicadores IBGE. Indicadores IBGE—Pesquisa Nacional por Amostra de Domicílios Contínua Divulgação Especial Medidas de Subutilização da Força de Trabalho no Brasil. Rio de Janeiro: IBGE.

IBGE—Instituto Brasileiro de Geografia e Estatística. 2019. *Pesquisa Nacional por Amostra de Domicílios Contínua*. Notas técnicas. Versão 1.6. Rio de Janeiro: IBGE.

IMF—International Monetary Fund. 2020, October. *World economic outlook reports*. Washington, DC: World Economic Outlook.

Krein, J. D. 2018. O desmonte dos direitos, as novas configurações do trabalho e o esvaziamento da ação coletiva: consequências da reforma trabalhista. *Tempo social*, 30(1): 77–104.

Kurt, R. 2019. Industry 4.0 in Terms of Industrial Relations and Its Impacts on Labor Life. *Procedia Computer Science*, 158: 590–601.

Luque, C. A., Silber, S. D., Luna, F. V., & Zagha, R. 2020. *Reagindo à crise— Não faz sentido diferenciar problemas de liquidez de problemas de solvência.*

Disponível abr. 13, 2020, em, https://valor.globo.com/opiniao/coluna/reagindo-a-crise.ghtml.

Menezes, F. N. A., Cabanas, P. H. F., & Komatsu, B. K. 2014. Tendências recentes do mercado de trabalho brasileiro. In *Mercado de trabalho: conjuntura e análise.* Instituto de Pesquisa Econômica Aplicada; Ministério do Trabalho e Emprego, Ano 20 (fevereiro 2014). Brasília: Ipea, MTE.

MTE—Brasil. 2019, Agosto de. *Cadastro Geral de Empregados e Desempregados (CAGED)*. **Lei N. ° 4.923/65 Sumário Executivo.**

OIT—Organización Internacional del Trabajo. 2020. *Nota técnica—Impactos en el mercado de trabajo y los ingresos en América Latina y el Caribe*. Panorama Laboral en tiempos de la COVID-19.

Pastore, A. C. 2020, 12 abr. Precisamos de ousadia e responsabilidade. *O Estado de S. Paulo*. Disponível abr. 12, 2020, em, https://digital.estadao. com.br/o-estado-de-s-paulo/20200412.

Riminucci, M. 2018. Industry 4.0 and human resources development: A view from Japan. *E-Journal of International and Comparative Labor Studies*, 7(1).

Wright, C. F., Wailes, N., Bamber, G. J., & Lansbury, R. D. 2017. Beyond national systems, towards a "gig economy"? A research agenda for international and comparative employment relations. *Employee Responsibilities and Rights Journal*, 29(4): 247–257.

4 Talent Management in the Interface Between Cultural Heritage and Modernity

A Case Study of Younger Mexican Middle Managers in a Regional Office

Jacobo Ramirez and Anne-Marie Søderberg

Introduction

The younger generation—those born after 1980, often termed "millennials"—represents one of the fastest-growing segments in the job market (Fry, 2016). Some multinational corporations (MNCs) have revised their human resource (HR) strategies to attract this group, appealing to their expectations for skill development, rapid advancement, and a better work/life balance (Ng, Lyons, & Schweitzer, 2017). Attracting and retaining young and highly educated managers (Petrucelli, 2017) with international business management experience is even more challenging in emerging markets such as Mexico because both foreign and domestic companies compete strongly for local talent (e.g., Newburry, Gardberg, & Sanchez, 2014) due to the prevalence of foreign direct investment (FDI) (World Bank, 2020).

This chapter builds on a longitudinal study of how Arla Foods, a Scandinavian dairy MNC, established its Latin American office in Mexico City and staffed it with young local talent. Surprisingly, Arla Foods succeeded in attracting—and retaining—a number of highly educated younger Mexicans with experience in international business, despite the company and its products not being known in Mexico. We investigate the following questions: What are the emerging work motivators of middle managers in Mexico, and what management practices can be adopted to retain them?

We suggest that Mexican middle managers were attracted to Arla Foods because they expected less supervision and intervention from Danish expatriate managers than they would from Mexican superiors and envisioned more opportunities for professional development through a participative management style characterized by trust, empowerment, and delegation of responsibility. Moreover, we suggest that they were attracted by the

working conditions, which offered a better work/life balance and more flexibility than they would find at Mexican companies, where employees are
typically expected to work long hours (OECD, 2020). In the regional office,
they experienced more dialogue and feedback within their team, which they
considered a community of equals.

Below, we present the chosen theoretical framework for this study regarding key international HR management (HRM) issues related to recruiting
and retaining local talent in a transnational context. We draw on insights
from international business research on MNCs in emerging markets, from
studies of "millennial" employees, and from current debates regarding
globally standardized HR policies and practices versus local adaptation and
responsiveness. Next, the chosen research methodology and case organization are presented, and the specificities of the research context are described.
We then offer an interpretation and discussion of our empirical findings and
conclude by emphasizing the contributions of our case study for practice
and suggesting areas for future study.

Theoretical Framework

Several international HRM scholars claim that globalization enables standardized practices to be smoothly and effectively transferred from an MNC
to its subsidiaries. Other scholars take a critical stance when arguing that
"global best practices" actually represent a "dominance effect, a tendency
of following and learning a role model . . . stemming from a country that
occupies a dominant position in a hierarchy of national economies" (Chung,
Sparrow, & Bozkurt, 2014, p. 557).

Some scholars argue that practices developed in one institutional and cultural context cannot be easily adapted to another (Kaufman, 2016). Both
scholars and practitioners may exhibit "naïve optimism" based on a universalist paradigm (Farndale et al., 2017) by "generally assum[ing] that MNCs
want to standardize practices wherever they can but are prevented from
doing so by local circumstances" (Brewster, Mayrhofer, & Smale, 2016,
p. 286). Other scholars (Bonache, Trullen, & Sanchez, 2012; Dávila &
Elvira, 2012, 2015) strongly recommend a more context-sensitive approach
to HR issues that considers environmental complexity and the historical
development of society.

When companies try to let management ideas, tools, and practices travel
(Czarniawska-Joerges & Sevón, 2005) to offices in different sociocultural
contexts, we expect that hybrid HRM policies and practices will be developed (Chung et al., 2014; Yousfi, 2014). We suggest that local employees will inevitably *interpret* the "global standards" and "best practices"
and, sometimes based on conflict, *negotiate* with expatriates and other

representatives from headquarters (HQ) as to what should be considered good workplace behavior, drawing on their respective values, expectations, and cultural preferences (Ramirez & Søderberg, 2020). In our case, which focuses on the path from a Scandinavian HQ to a regional office in Mexico, the cross-cultural interaction of HR ideas and practices takes place in the specific organizational and national context of a regional office of a Scandinavian MNC when expatriate managers and Mexican middle managers *interpret* and *negotiate* these standards and practices.

Although national and organizational cultures and related management practices change over time, not least in the era of globalization, we acknowledge that certain forms of continuity can persist as a framework of meaning (d'Iribarne, 2002) that may guide the interpretations of local actors of a specific cultural community, providing them with "acceptable ways of organizing and regulating social life" (Yousfi, 2014, p. 398). The following sections present several management ideas and practices that are observed in Mexican and Scandinavian societal contexts to provide a contextualized understanding of what tends to be recognized as "acceptable ways" of managing and working together. We acknowledge that there will be differences among firms in both regions based on industry dynamics, company strategy, and specific corporate culture. In the case studied, it is obvious that both cultural preferences and preferred management practices distinguish Mexican employees from employees in Scandinavia.

Management in Mexico

Recent GLOBE studies (Chhokar, Brodbeck, & House, 2007; House, Hanges, Javidan, Dorfman, & Gupta, 2004; Howell et al., 2007) focusing on national cultural values and related leadership styles suggest that Latin American managers prefer to act as autocratic leaders with unquestioned power and top-down decision-making (Martínez, 2003). This "paternalistic" leadership style emerged in privately owned farms (*haciendas*), wherein the owner and boss (*patrón*) provided food, housing, and medical care to workers and their families, as well as education for their children (Brumley, 2014; Dávila & Elvira, 2012). The workers met the *hacienda*'s need for a stable workforce and received support, protection, and care for themselves and their families in return. This encouraged workers to develop an emotional attachment to the hacienda, and it created a structure of strong familial community, with high degrees of loyalty (Brumley, 2014, p. 469).

Dávila and Elvira (2012) suggested that most managers in Mexico still favor caring for individual employees as part of a collective social structure in which everyone collaborates according to their designated status and role. The strong social bonds created between traditional Mexican superiors and their subordinates generate a platform for psychological dependency and mutual loyalty (Dávila & Elvira, 2015; Litrico, 2007) and explain why traditional Mexican companies are often described as being similar to family-owned businesses (Dávila & Elvira, 2015). Indeed, many Mexican companies still function as social institutions that compensate for the lack of institutional support and protection in Mexican society.

However, because of globalization and increased FDI in Mexico (World Bank, 2020), an egalitarian and humanistic leadership style has emerged in which Mexican companies attempt to provide care and social support for their employees while also ensuring gender equality in the workplace (Brumley, 2014; Paludi, Salvador, & Albert, 2020). This emerging humanistic leadership style aims to improve individual performance by focusing on training to meet the company's needs when collaborating with foreign partners in a globalized business context.

The interlink between historical colonial patterns with "modern" management and leadership styles places local employees in what some scholars term a polycultural setting, where "cultural influence[s] on individuals [are] partial and plural and cultural traditions interact and change each other" (Morris, Chiu, & Liu, 2015, p. 634). Morris et al. (2015, p. 634) argue that polyculturalism "focuses on how people live coherent lives informed by multiple legacies, how they borrow from or react against foreign [influences], with ripple effects within their communities." This understanding is close to what we and other scholars have termed "hybridity" in a postcolonial business context (Ramirez & Søderberg, 2020; Yousfi, 2014).

Management in Scandinavia

In the GLOBE studies on national cultural values and related leadership styles, the Nordic countries of Denmark, Norway, and Sweden all score low on "power distance" and high on "participation in decision-making" (Chhokar et al., 2007). Managers in Scandinavia tend to downplay their authority and prefer more egalitarian practices, delegating responsibility to subordinates and involving employees in idea generation; this is often termed a "participative" leadership style. The Danish education system explicitly teaches students that they should think independently and be critical of authority (teachers, bosses, doctors, and politicians, among others), and students are encouraged to question an authority if they disagree with its decisions. This approach creates self-confidence and results in only modest respect for authority. At work, Danes enjoys a high degree of flexibility, such as flexible start times and the option of working from home.

It is important to emphasize that Scandinavian countries have not always been so "democratic" and "egalitarian." Østergård (2012) offers a historical frame of reference for the preferred values and behavior of many Danish business people and identifies the egalitarian practices of the social-democratic universal welfare state as a profound influence on the thoughts and actions of many Danes since the late 1920s, such as their perspectives on caring for weaker members of a community. A high level of interpersonal trust is evident in Denmark, and societal concern for other people's needs is considered essential. Similar to how companies in Mexico support employees and their families, the Danish welfare state offers publicly financed education, health care, and social insurance schemes to all citizens.

Millennials

The term "millennials" is often applied to people born between the early 1980s and mid-1990s (Ng et al., 2017). A common denominator is their middle-class upbringing in a period characterized by the globalization of culture and commerce and a more liberal approach to authority and societal norms and values than their highly engaged and hardworking parents. The widespread use of digital technologies and social media is another characteristic shared by many members of this group (Hatum, 2013).

Western scholars have made many claims regarding the "universal truths" that pertain to millennials and their dominant psychological dispositions and attitudes toward work, career, and life, but these claims are often based on studies of primarily white teenagers and college students (e.g., Graybill, 2014). Western consultants also provide lists of the common characteristics of this generation, who have now entered the workforce, to guide companies in their adaptation of various HRM activities to meet millennials' aspirations and expectations (Buckley, Viechnicki, & Barua, 2015). Below, we present the key workplace priorities of Western millennials, emphasizing that these characteristics are dependent on the societal, economic, and social conditions in which these young people grew up and that the Mexican millennials in our case study may have other priorities.

With a high degree of self-esteem and self-confidence, millennials are very concerned about their opportunities for career progression through rapid promotions (Ng, Schweitzer, & Lyons, 2010). They expect employers to offer them job security and a good working environment with a positive atmosphere. They want to be challenged at work but not overstressed. They tend to prefer workplaces with a flat hierarchy that allows more immediate feedback from superiors and peers. Millennials look for meaningful and fulfilling work, driven by a desire to make the world a better place (Deloitte Global, 2020). They thus tend to leave an organization if their employers do not focus sufficiently on "people and purpose" (Buckley et al., 2015) or if their needs for personal freedom and autonomy are not met (Deloitte

Table 4.1 Sample Information on the Interviewees

Employee Position	Age (in 2017)	Nationality	Interview Location(s)
(1) Regional Director LATAM	37	Danish	Copenhagen, Mexico City
(2) Business Development Manager	41	Danish	Copenhagen, Mexico City
(3) Administrative Assistant	37	Mexican	Mexico City
(4) Senior Manager	37	Mexican	Mexico City
(5) Export Assistant	41	Mexican	Mexico City
(6) Export Manager	43	Mexican	Mexico City (Phone interview)
(7) Senior Regional Category Manager	37	Mexican	Mexico City
(8) Regional Category Manager	35	Mexican	Mexico City
(9) Regional Category Manager	43	Mexican	Mexico City
(10) Head of Business Development	45	Danish	Copenhagen
(11) Sales Manager: Mexico	45	Danish	Copenhagen, Mexico City
(12) Sales Manager: Central America	37	Danish	Mexico City
(13) HR Assistant	30	Danish	Copenhagen

Global, 2020). Millennials have high expectations regarding flexible working arrangements that allow them to balance work and private life, including time for hobbies and other leisure activities (Ng et al., 2010).

In our analysis, we examine how these characteristics compare to the expectations and ideals voiced by Mexican middle managers in the regional office of a Scandinavian MNC, who grew up in significantly different socio-cultural contexts than Western millennials but still had better opportunities than previous generations to receive higher education (OECD, 2020). Many of them are strictly classed as millennials, although a few were born slightly before 1980 (see Table 4.1).

Methodology

Arla Foods is a Scandinavian MNC that is cooperatively owned by 12,500 farmers (Arla Foods, 2016a). In the 1880s, Danish and Swedish milk farmers created cooperatives to invest in joint dairy production facilities. Over time, the idea of a democratically managed cooperative proved increasingly attractive, and the company expanded from the local to the national level and eventually to the regional level in Europe (Arla Foods, 2016a, 2017). The consolidation of Arla Foods as a multinational dairy company within the European Union was followed by the establishment of regional offices in the Middle East, Africa, Russia, China, Southeast Asia, and Latin America, with the goal of intensifying the worldwide distribution of Arla Foods' products.

In our case study, various qualitative methods were used to study Arla Foods' regional office in Mexico. The first author conducted semistructured, face-to-face interviews in English and Spanish with top managers from Denmark and middle managers from Mexico (see Table 4.1) over a period of three years (2014–2016). Several interviews were performed at the HQ in Denmark, although the majority was conducted at the regional office in Mexico. All interviews were recorded and transcribed. The interviews constitute the primary data for this case analysis and are supplemented with field notes and participant observations.

Several company documents (annual reports, strategy chapters, job advertisements, etc.) and media texts were downloaded from Arla Foods' website, thereby providing opportunities for data triangulation. Our coding of the interviews was an analytical process in which we shifted our attention between the primary data (interviews, observations) and secondary data (previous reports on HRM policies and management practices in Mexico and Denmark and literature on millennials).

Empirical Findings

Staffing the Regional Office

The Latin American office in Mexico City, denoted as LATAM, was established in 2013. Two Danish managers were sent to LATAM from Arla Foods' HQ, and two other Danish managers were relocated from a sales office in the Dominican Republic. These managers are multilingual and highly proficient in Spanish and English.

The regional director at LATAM stated in 2013 that "*the challenge in opening a regional office in Mexico was not the legal procedures but attracting candidates to work at LATAM,*" because neither Arla Foods nor its products were known in Mexico. The regional director further commented on the employment dynamics in Mexico, which may play a role in attracting and retaining Mexican employees:

> *The [Mexican] economy is doing well in a global context. That means wages are going up and unemployment is low [among highly educated talent]. It also means that employees can easily jump from one company to another.*

The recruitment process followed Arla Foods' global standard. The first job advertisement was posted in 2013 on the Arla Foods' webpage for a position as a business development manager. The job advertisement emphasized that the preferred leadership style entailed delegating responsibility and empowering employees to make decisions; in addition, it highlighted future career opportunities:

> *This is an excellent opportunity to set your mark on the market strategies for an entire region while building a platform for a future international career in Arla Foods. . . . You have strong analytical skills, a strategic mindset and a mature project management toolbox that enable you to lead projects independently with limited supervision.*

The regional director also used other methods of attracting applicants. "*I started asking my local partner for recommendations in order to hire Mexican employees. I also looked into LinkedIn and dealt with a recruitment agency.*"

In a follow-up interview in 2014, the regional director reflected on the need to recruit local people with optimal job profiles:

> *We mainly seek local people . . . We are confident that we can reach our goals (. . ., and it [requires] local people with insight in the Latin American market. Knowledge and [understanding] of Arla Foods— that does not worry me. It can be learned. But we have to localize and tropicalize, and that is done with Mexicans and other locals.*

By March 2016, LATAM had employed seven Mexican middle managers with experience working in international and local firms in the food industry (employees 3–9 in Table 4.1). They had all graduated from bachelor's degree programs at prestigious private business schools in Mexico, and many of them had completed studies at the postgraduate level and were enrolled in specialization programs in Mexico and Spain.

The process of selecting Mexican employees appears to reflect Arla Foods' strategy, as explained by the head of business development and commercial operations at Arla Foods' HQ in 2014:

> *they must be in their specific functional domains, very strong high caliber people. So, for finance, I want one of the best finance people. For business development strategy, I need entrepreneurs. I need people who are willing to take risks and who are not, as I call it, just boxed in. Saying, "I just do finance. I just do HR" [is no good].*

Another Danish senior manager at LATAM confirmed that, in many ways, Mexican employees were ready to adapt and grow in new directions and bridge boundaries: "*I think the team here (at LATAM) consists of people who are in-between, [who] can be changed, because I have already seen [it] happen.*"

Onboarding Process

In 2016, the regional director explained the process they had used to onboard and integrate the Mexican middle managers into the multicultural team at LATAM.

> *We have a policy that there is a talk after a week, after a month, and after three months. It is the part of "onboarding" and integration in Arla Foods.*

The onboarding program included a visit to Arla Foods' HQ in Denmark, where the Mexican middle managers met their colleagues at HQ and visited the farmers and milk processing sites. Statements from Danish senior managers and Mexican employees confirmed that the objective of the visit to HQ was to develop employees' holistic understanding of Arla Foods and enable them to identify with Arla Foods and embrace the brand. A Mexican employee described her experience of the visit:

> *What struck me . . . was that [I got] an overview of the whole process, not only production but also the origin of the raw material and the products that I'm selling. I have not experienced [that] in other companies. When I was selling cereal [her former job] . . . I did not know where the cereal came from, how it was harvested, I did not know anything. [But here] I was informed . . . "we do this and that, . . . this is how we feed the cows, what happens after the milk comes out, where and how the processes occur." Here, I get to know the whole value chain, [which] I really like.*
>
> (Regional Category Manager)

Arla Foods' corporate values and preferred behaviors are presented in more detail in the following sections, where examples are given regarding how Mexican employees interpret and enact them on a daily basis.

Trust, Flexibility, and Autonomy

In an interview in 2014, the Danish regional director for Latin America emphasized that his management style at LATAM was primarily inspired by the corporate values (e.g., trust, flexibility, autonomy, and work/life balance) and preferred behaviors (e.g., promoting initiative and being proactive) practiced at Arla Foods' HQ: "*We are a European company, and we bring the values of Arla Foods [to Mexico]. I feel my Mexican employees like them.*" He stated that he trusts his employees and therefore accepts flexible schedules, as long as the job is completed and performed well. For example, some Mexican employees live some distance away from the office in Mexico City and to avoid traffic, they prefer to start work very early. He therefore provided all staff members with a key to the entrance so that they can start working when it fits their individual schedules.

He formalized this working routine by introducing an "intense work schedule," whereby employees work from 7:00 to 14:00 without major breaks. The explanation provided for this work schedule was that commuting employees could avoid traffic jams and arrive home in time for dinner with their families. Nevertheless, this "intense work schedule" is not compulsory. The freedom offered to employees to adjust their work schedules echoes Arla Foods' Code of Conduct, which "*applies to all employees, and it is the role of our leaders to ensure that a culture of responsibility is embedded*" (Arla Foods, 2016a, p. 3).

Trust and relative autonomy to decide responsibly are values that Mexican employees at LATAM highly appreciate. For example, a Mexican middle manager explained that she was relieved to no longer be micromanaged by a superior, as she had experienced at other MNCs in Mexico. Moreover, at LATAM, her colleagues listen to her ideas and discuss them openly with her. It gradually improved her self-confidence and motivation to learn:

> [At LATAM,] the people trust me because I argue well, because I know what I'm doing. Thus, when a company trusts you, that's when you learn . . . it makes you grow and makes you feel good.
>
> (Senior Regional Category Manager)

Feedback and Dialogue

The regional director at LATAM emphasized that feedback and dialogue are important for ensuring good employee performance but that employees in Denmark and Mexico expected different styles of feedback. In a Scandinavian business context, feedback often implies very direct communication regarding what is good and what deserves critique, while Mexican employees are used to a less direct approach. A Mexican manager confirmed that "*[here at LATAM, management is] very direct and open.*" Although this direct communication style may be somewhat new to Mexican employees, they gradually come to appreciate it because it is considered to be a tool for developing the workplace into a community of equals who can grow together.

According to Arla Foods' Code of Conduct, "*trust is a prerequisite for responsible business. Regardless of where in the world, we want to have an open and transparent relationship with our consumers, customers, competitors, business partners and other stakeholders. We do this by communicating openly and maintaining a continuous dialogue*" (Arla Foods, 2016a, p. 10). The regional director further explained that Arla Foods intends to create a strong feedback culture in somewhat self-driving teams; thus, dialogue is encouraged (Arla Foods, 2016b) and used to assess employee performance. The process of engaging in constant dialogue and feedback requires a certain awareness of the differences between the Danish and Mexican preferences for direct and indirect communication, respectively. The principles in the Code of Conduct may be shared across cultures, but to be sustainable, the practices need to be adapted to the local context (Bonache et al., 2012; Ramirez & Søderberg, 2020).

The two Danish managers at LATAM understood that their direct communication style may be perceived as somewhat aggressive and face-threatening by Mexican employees. Consequently, they attempt to be more polite than they would toward Danish employees and make an effort to communicate in a less straightforward manner, especially when evaluating an outcome, to avoid silencing and offending their Mexican colleagues.

The two Danish managers expressed that they had not observed any strong tensions between the Danes and Mexicans at the LATAM office. However, they wondered whether the Mexican employees always conveyed the information necessary for good and effective collaboration across national divides or if they sometimes tried to avoid conflict. They have experienced that silence in a Mexican context does not necessarily mean acceptance and have formed what some might consider a stereotypical view of Mexicans. Nevertheless, they have developed new ways of asking questions based on this perception to determine if their Mexican employees understand—and agree—with their suggestions:

> *You have to say [in Mexico], "But what do you think about this? Do you agree?" "No, I don't." "Why?" You have to ask a lot of times to make sure that the people understand and also agree with what you suggest, because otherwise, you could leave a meeting and say, "Okay, guys, we had a great meeting and we all agreed," [and afterwards realize] "No, we did not."*
>
> (Danish Sales Manager)

The communication within the multicultural team at LATAM thus appears to be supported by managerial efforts to empower Mexican employees and allow them to voice their opinions more freely than they have been accustomed to.

Hierarchy and Empowerment

The Danish regional director considers the staff at LATAM as a community of peers and attempts to "*break down hierarchies and create fellowship,*" as advocated at the leadership seminars at Arla Foods' HQ.

To build a more "friendly" work environment at LATAM and strengthen team building, the regional director has, for example, introduced a weekly breakfast. Every Wednesday at 9:00 a.m., all employees sit together around a table and eat dark rye bread with butter and slices of yellow cheese. This breakfast setting is an occasion to talk about private issues, such as life outside the workplace and to comment on daily news or local sports events. As a Mexican participant observer, this purely Danish breakfast ritual with Arla Foods' dairy products was somewhat peculiar, considering that it occurs at a time of the day when Mexicans would normally gather and eat tacos with minced meat, vegetables, spiced sauce, and perhaps some grated and melted cheese. However, weekly breakfast is well attended and appreciated as a method of forming a community of peers. Indirectly, the breakfasts also support Arla Foods' management ideal of close and daily collaboration: "*to succeed, we work together—to Lead, Sense & Create*" (Arla Foods job advertisement).

Mexican Employee Expectations of Paternalistic Management

Although Arla Foods' values and management practices are greatly appreciated by the younger middle managers, as illustrated by the quotes earlier, some voiced contrasting expectations for a more traditional superior–subordinate relationship: "*The leader, he is the one to guide us and show the direction in which we are going to move*" (Mexican Business Development Manager). The Mexican middle managers seem to appreciate the work life at LATAM, yet some also advocate for a more traditional superior–subordinate relationship and wish that the regional manager exerts "directive management" and care not only for employees but also for their families.

A Mexican employee at LATAM had broken her ankle outside the workplace and voiced serious doubts regarding how the regional director would address this emergency. She was relieved to discover that Arla Foods not only "*cares for the environment*" but also "*cares at every step*" for their employees, as the company claims on its corporate website. This caring behavior was combined with her superior's flexible attitude regarding *where* and *when* work is performed, as long as the tasks were accomplished.

This flexibility is less common in traditional Mexican firms, where employees are expected to work in the office during a fixed period.

Compensation System

The Mexican employees also raised concerns regarding the lack of a compensation system at LATAM, which we see as an indication of their understanding of paternalistic management. According to our interviewees, other foreign MNCs in Mexico offer generous nonmonetary incentives such as paid meals, transport bonuses, and private health insurance. The Mexican employees also mentioned that salary is not their first motivator for working at LATAM:

> *In regard to the benefits, . . . Nestlé . . . and other companies in Mexico City had better ones. However, it was a trade-off . . . my priorities were, first, a challenging job; second, a good work/life balance; and third, a good salary.*
>
> (Senior Regional Category Manager)

In a follow-up interview in 2016, we found that the very first Mexican who was hired at LATAM in 2014 as an export manager for South America left for a subsidiary of a US firm based in Mexico City. We contacted him to learn why he left LATAM.

> *I changed because . . . I did not have a good [nonmonetary compensation] package. I had only the salary. Being a global company, all employees should have the same benefits as in Europe or benefits that can compete in the local market and compensation that is higher than what is stipulated by the law, for example, insurance for medical expenses, vouchers to buy groceries, bonuses, etc. Now . . . , what I miss from LATAM is the Danish culture—responsibility, hardworking, punctual, direct—and that you can propose ideas and be proactive in business development.*

The regional director explained that "*LATAM is a small regional office that does not have the infrastructure to provide compensation packages like other MNCs in Mexico.*" However, the regional director did not openly question the global HR standards set by HQ.

Discussion

As documented in Table 4.1, most employees recruited to the multicultural management team at LATAM were younger Mexicans born after 1980.

They had worked for local and foreign MNCs and studied at prestigious private business schools in Mexico, where they also learned about global HRM policies and practices. Thus, they do not identify only with Mexican societal values and may differentiate themselves from other Mexican employees as "foreign locals" (Caprar, 2011). Their attitudes and behavior may be understood through the lens of polyculturalism, since it describes how their experiences span across different cultural traditions and how they identify with parts of Arla Foods' organizational culture (e.g., Morris et al., 2015).

The focus of our research is on the emerging work motivators of talented young managers in LATAM and the management practices adopted to retain them in the regional office of the Scandinavian MNC. Some Mexican employees were particularly attracted by the emphasis in the job advertisement on limited supervision and intervention from superiors, which could be interpreted as dimensions of participative management (Chhokar et al., 2007). The expectation that a Scandinavian MNC would offer a better work/life balance than a Mexican company also seems to have encouraged applicants.

We asked about the management practices adopted to retain the Mexican middle managers at LATAM. Our results suggest that trust was built within the multicultural team during the onboarding process and reinforced in other ways later on, e.g., by offering employees flexible working hours and delegating responsibility. This empowered the employees and encouraged them to make decisions without constant supervision and intervention. These Scandinavian management practices—combined with an emphasis on dialogue and direct feedback—appear to be strongly aligned with millennials' desire for a flatter hierarchy, less formal power vested in authorities, and room to develop their skills and competencies to quickly advance their careers—even internationally—within the MNC (e.g., Ng et al., 2017).

These empirical findings are in line with other studies on the attractiveness of foreign firms as employers in Latin America (Newburry et al., 2014) and suggest that MNCs from more egalitarian societies such as Denmark may be particularly attractive to younger Mexicans because of their focus on empowerment and participative management. Moreover, Arla Foods provided opportunities for their Mexican middle managers to strongly identify with its corporate values, its production of dairy products ("*from cow to table*"), and its corporate brand.

However, Mexican middle managers at LATAM voiced concerns about the absence of nonmonetary compensation packages, particularly healthcare services, for themselves and their families. These critical voices were not considered by the Danish regional director, who expressed that the Scandinavian MNC's global HR standards and policies were sound and fair.

He was able and ready to adapt to the local environment in many other areas due to his in-depth understanding of the Mexican business context, but he did not display any flexibility toward the local expectation and need for a nonmonetary compensation system. It seems that the regional director did not have the power to influence and change Arla Foods' global HR policies.

Previous studies (e.g., Caligiuri, Lepak, & Bonache, 2010) have indicated that HR practices such as "benefits" are more adaptable to the local context; our case suggests an exception. Failing to adapt to the expectation of nonmonetary compensation may be a latent obstacle to attracting and retaining talented Mexican employees because Mexican society does not provide the same degree of social security as Scandinavian welfare states. Mexican employees' psychological dependency on their immediate superior as a "caring father" and their financial dependency on the firm as an "extended family" have been discussed previously in studies on Latin America as a kinship society with a humanistic leadership style (Dávila & Elvira, 2012, 2015; Velez-Calle, Robledo-Ardila, & Rodriguez-Rios, 2015). Our study illustrates that a lack of "financial care" may be a challenge for foreign subsidiaries to retain talent among Mexican middle managers.

As documented earlier, autonomy, flexibility, and a better work/life balance appear to be strong motivators for younger Mexicans employed in the regional office. They had left local companies or foreign MNCs despite receiving compensation packages that included private health care, life insurance, gym membership, and coupons for groceries, among other benefits. Such benefits, in addition to a workplace infrastructure with access to secretary arranging travel plans, among other things, were often offered to Mexican middle managers. However, our findings indicate that the younger Mexicans in our sample were ready, at least in the short term, to give up these benefits in favor of a more egalitarian work environment that offers flexible work schedules and perhaps even career opportunities at other locations within the MNC. The Mexican middle managers felt that they could grow personally while developing their managerial skills in this international business setting.

Concluding Remarks

This case study focuses on the historic and sociocultural context for various HR policies and practices and presents insights into the expectations and desires of younger Mexican talent, which are similar to the expectations of millennials in Western countries (e.g., Ng et al., 2010, 2017). Our empirical findings from Mexico are valuable for both domestic and foreign firms because they suggest that employers can develop strategies to attract and retain younger employees and gain their trust and loyalty if they are aware of country-specific work conditions and generational preferences. Our empirical findings suggest that younger Mexican middle managers may be willing to sacrifice, at least temporarily, a robust compensation system in the local job market to gain a better work/life balance and advance their professional development and international career opportunities.

Nevertheless, some interview statements indicated that a paternalistic leadership style still shapes Mexicans' expectations of managerial behavior to a certain extent. This persistent continuity (d'Iribarne, 2002; Yousfi, 2014) may explain why even highly educated younger Mexicans with international work experience share some cultural influences from the colonial legacy and voice expectations of a caring boss. Despite their preferences for a better work/life balance, more autonomy, empowerment, etc., they are still socialized within a sociocultural context that promotes an understanding of the workplace as a family with strong social bonds between the employer and employee (e.g., Brumley, 2014; Dávila & Elvira, 2015). This hybridity in attitudes and behavior must be considered when dealing with HRM issues in a Latin American sociocultural context.

References

Arla Foods. 2016a. *Arla code of conduct 2016*. Retrieved March 22, 2017, from http://docs.arla.com/CodeofConduct/EN/.

Arla Foods. 2016b. *Arla foods corporate strategy—good growth 2020*. Retrieved November 28, 2016, from www.arla.com/company/strategy/strategy-2020/overview/

Arla Foods. 2017. *Care in every step-arla*. Retrieved March 29, 2017, from www.arla.com/company/farmer-owned/care-in-every-step/.

Bonache, J., Trullen, J., & Sanchez, J. I. 2012. Managing cross-cultural differences: Testing human resource models in Latin America. *Journal of Business Research,* 65: 1773–1781.

Brewster, C., Mayrhofer, W., & Smale, A. 2016. Crossing the streams: HRM in multinational enterprises and comparative HRM. *Human Resource Management Review,* 26: 285–297.

Brumley, K. M. 2014. 'You care for your work; I'll care for your family': Perceptions of paternalistic managerial actions and employee commitment in Mexico. *Community, Work & Family,* 17: 467–485.

Buckley, P., Viechnicki, P., & Barua, A. 2015. *Understanding millennials and generational differences*. Retrieved March 11, 2017, from https://dupress.deloitte.com/dup-us-en/economy/issues-by-the-numbers/understanding-millennials-generational-differences.html.

Caligiuri, P., Lepak, D., & Bonache, J. 2010. *Managing the global workforce. Global dimensions of business*. Hoboken, NJ: Wiley-Blackwell.

Caprar, D. V. 2011. Foreign locals: A cautionary tale on the culture of MNC local employees. *Journal of International Business Studies,* 42: 608–628.

Chhokar, J. S., Brodbeck, F. C., & House, R. J. 2007. *Culture and leadership across the world: The GLOBE book of in-depth studies of 25 societies*. Mahwah, NJ: Lawrence Erlbaum Associates.

Chung, C., Sparrow, P., & Bozkurt, Ö. 2014. South Korean MNEs' International HRM approach: Hybridization of global standards and local practices. *Journal of World Business*, 49: 549–559.

Czarniawska-Joerges, B., & Sevón, G. 2005. *Global ideas: How ideas, objects and practices travel in a global economy*. Lund and Copenhagen: Liber & Copenhagen Business School Press.

Dávila, A., & Elvira, M. B. 2015. HRM in a kinship society: The case of Latin America. In F. Horwitz & P. Budhwar (Eds.), *Handbook of human resource management in emerging markets* (pp. 372–392). Cheltenham, UK: Edward Elgar Publishing.

Dávila, A., & Elvira, M. M. 2012. Humanistic leadership: Lessons from Latin America. *Journal of World Business*, 47: 548–554.

Deloitte Global. 2020. *The Deloitte global millennial survey 2020: Millennials and Gen Zs hold the key to creating a "better normal"*. Retrieved October 13, 2020, from https://www2.deloitte.com/global/en/pages/about-deloitte/articles/millennialsurvey.html.

d'Iribarne, P. 2002. Motivating workers in emerging countries: Universal tools and local adaptations. *Journal of Organizational Behavior*, 23: 243–256.

Farndale, E., Raghuram, S., Gully, S., Liu, X., Phillips, J. M., & Vidović, M. 2017. A vision of international HRM research. *The International Journal of Human Resource Management*, 28: 1625–1639.

Fry, R. 2016. *Millennials overtake baby boomers as America's largest generation*. Retrieved March 11, 2017, from https://pewrsr.ch/1UcT1B3.

Graybill, J. O. 2014. Millennials among the professional workforce in academic libraries: Their perspective on leadership. *The Journal of Academic Librarianship*, 40: 10–15.

Hatum, A. 2013. Attracting millennials to the workplace. In A. Hatum (Ed.), *The new workforce challenge: How today's leading companies are adapting to the future* (pp. 63–98). London: Palgrave Macmillan.

House, R. J., Hanges, P. J., Javidan, M., Dorfman, P. W., & Gupta, V. 2004. *Culture, leadership, and organizations: The GLOBE study of 62 societies*. London: Sage Publications.

Howell, J. P., DelaCerda, J., Martínez, S. M., Prieto, L., Bautista, J. A., Ortiz, J., Dorfman, P., & Méndez, M. J. 2007. Leadership and culture in Mexico. *Journal of World Business*, 42: 449–462.

Kaufman, B. E. 2016. Globalization and convergence—divergence of HRM across nations: New measures, explanatory theory, and non-standard predictions from bringing in economics. *Human Resource Management Review*, 26: 338–351.

Litrico, J. B. 2007. Beyond paternalism: Cross-cultural perspectives on the functioning of a Mexican production plant. *Journal of Business Ethics*, 73(1): 53–63.

Martínez, P. G. 2003. Paternalism as a positive form of leader—subordinate exchange: Evidence from Mexico. *Management Research*, 1: 227–242.

Morris, M. W., Chiu, C. Y., & Liu, Z. 2015. Polycultural psychology. *Annual Review of Psychology,* 66(1): 631–659.

Newburry, W., Gardberg, N. A., & Sanchez, J. I. 2014. Employer attractiveness in Latin America: The association among Foreignness, Internationalization and Talent Recruitment. *Journal of International Management,* 20: 327–344.

Ng, E. S. W., Lyons, S. T., & Schweitzer, L. 2017. Millennials in Canada: Young workers in a challenging labour market. In E. Parry & J. McCarthy (Eds.), *The Palgrave handbook of age diversity and work* (pp. 325–344). London: Palgrave Macmillan.

Ng, E. S. W., Schweitzer, L., & Lyons, S. T. 2010. New generation, great expectations: A field study of the millennial generation. *Journal of Business and Psychology,* 25(2): 281–292.

OECD. 2020. *How's life? 2020: Measuring well-being.* Paris, France: OECD Publishing.

Østergård, U. 2012. Danish national identity: A historical account. In M. C. Gertsen, A. M. Søderberg, & M. Zølner (Eds.), *Global collaboration: Intercultural experiences and learning* (pp. 37–55). Basingstoke: Palgrave Macmillan.

Paludi, M. I., Salvador, B., & Albert, M. 2020. Women CEOs in Mexico: Gendered local/global divide and the diversity management discourse. *Critical Perspectives on International Business.* https://doi.org/10.1108/cpoib-08-2018-0071.

Petrucelli, T. 2017. Winning the "cat-and-mouse game" of retaining millennial talent. *Strategic HR Review,* 16: 42–44.

Ramirez, J., & Søderberg, A. M. 2020. Recontextualizing Scandinavian practices in a Latin American regional office. *Management Research,* 18: 99–119.

Velez-Calle, A., Robledo-Ardila, C., & Rodriguez-Rios, J. D. 2015. On the influence of interpersonal relations on business practices in Latin America: A comparison with the Chinese *Guanxi* and the Arab *Wasta. Thunderbird International Business Review,* 57: 281–293.

World Bank. 2020. *Foreign direct investment, net inflows (BoP, current US$) -Mexico (1970–2019).* Retrieved October 1, 2020, from https://data.worldbank.org/indicator/BX.KLT.DINV.CD.WD?locations=MX.

Yousfi, H. 2014. Rethinking hybridity in postcolonial contexts: What changes and what persists? The Tunisian case of Poulina's managers. *Organization Studies,* 35: 393–421.

5 Job, Career, and Calling of the Next Generation of the Family Firm

A Latin American Perspective

Pedro Vázquez, Luis Gómez Mejía and Milagros Molina

Introduction

Family firms are the prevalent form of economic and social organization around the world, particularly in Latin America. In this region, family control prevails not only in small firms but also in about 40% of the largest companies (Vázquez, 2017; Carrera, Vazquez, & Cornejo, 2019), with family firms representing by far the most important single important block of the region's GDP. The involvement of family members in the family firm can be observed in various leading corporate roles such as the shareholders assembly, the board of directors, and the top management team. This involvement is very high in Latin American family firms (Vazquez, Carrera, & Cornejo, 2020). Younger generations are likely to be incorporated in top decision-making positions in these Latin American firms in years to come. The development of abilities and interest of the next generation to continue work in the family firm is critical as it is likely to make a major difference on the future performance and even survival of these organizations (Sharma, Chrisman, Pablo, & Chua, 2001).

The systemic view of the family business proposes that sustainable performance has to be achieved and balanced considering the individual, the family, and the company (Habbershon, Williams, & MacMillan, 2003). The importance of individual fulfillment of the family member involved in the family firm in order for the system to be successful has been highlighted in the literature Perkins (2017). The kind of bond to work in the family firm may be experienced differently by the younger generations, and it is unclear whether most see this work as a job, a career, or a calling (Wrzesniewski, McCauley, Rozin, & Schwartz, 1997). The orientation experienced by the next generation of members of Latin American enterprising families to work in their family firms is a crucial issue as it is likely to influence the performance of the system at its various levels.

Family Firms in Latin America and Family Involvement in Leading Roles

As noted earlier, the family firm, a business entity that is controlled by one or more families, is a very relevant organizational form worldwide (Faccio & Lang, 2002; La Porta, Lopez-de-Silanes, & Shleifer, 1999), particularly in Latin America. This region represents about 9% of the world's population as well as 6% of the world's gross domestic product (GDP) and is the second most important emerging market in the world after Southeast Asia (Vassolo, De Castro, & Gomez-Mejia, 2011). Family firms are the prevalent form of economic and social organization in Latin America and contribute to approximately 60% of the region's GDP (IFERA, 2003). Family control prevails not only in small firms but also in about 40% of the largest companies of the region (Vázquez, 2017; Carrera et al., 2019). This prominence is evidenced in all countries of the region but with significant variability across countries as, for example, the national institutional context of Latin American countries affects competitiveness of family firms (Duran, van Essen, Heugens, Kostova, & Peng, 2019). Latin America shares several historical and cultural characteristics based on a common language, geographic roots, religion, class structure, and nature of authority (Lansberg & Perrow, 1991), and this context influences the way family firms are conceived, governed, and managed (Basco, 2015) as well as the behavior of enterprising families. In other words, strong commonalities may be observed across countries as a function of these shared cultural characteristics. For instance, the emphasis on centralization, hierarchy, patriarchism, and nepotism is a common denominator of family firms across the region.

The involvement of family members in the family firm can be observed in various leading corporate roles such as the shareholders assembly, the board of directors, and the top management team. This involvement will be affected by the intergenerational relationship and the generational succession process (Miller & Le Breton-Miller, 2006; Nordqvist, Sharma, & Chirico, 2014). The mentioned corporate governance bodies and roles function in a different way in the context of family firms because they have a more diverse set of goals and also because several of these goals are aimed at benefiting the controlling family as a key stakeholder (Vazquez & Rocha, 2018). Consistent with the literature family owners in Latin America strive to preserve their socioemotional wealth, which encompasses such aspects as control and influence, identification with the firm, social ties, emotional attachment, and dynastic succession (Gómez-Mejía, Haynes, Núñez-Nickel, Jacobson, & Moyano-Fuentes, 2007; Berrone, Cruz, & Gomez Mejía, 2012). This implies that controlling families pursue a combination of socioemotional goals that go beyond financial returns. This is reinforced by the fact that the involvement of family members in leading corporate positions in Latin America is high. Even in the very large firms, that usually employ several thousand nonfamily employees, in most cases the President of the firm is a family member and members of the boards and CEOs are family members in about 50% of cases (Vazquez et al., 2020). This prominent role of family members in positions with high influence in top decisions is even higher in smaller family enterprises.

Next Generation of Leaders of Enterprising Families

Although involvement of family members in top decision-making positions of Latin American family businesses is high, its nature and effect on the company will change over time due to the dynamic characteristics of the succession process (Nordqvist et al., 2014). About half of current family business leaders plan to retire between the ages of 61 and 70 (Calabrò & Valentino, 2019); emphasizing the need for an orderly succession process to transfer decision power as reflected in changes in ownership, direction and/ or management of the company. This succession usually involves a younger generation, the "next generation", that will have to take over the leadership of the family firm. This succession process can happen gradually, but sometimes also immediately, and can be organized or unexpected.

There may be currently up to five generations working together in the same family firm: the silent generation (born 1925–1945), baby boomers (born 1946–1964), generation X (born 1965–1980), millennials (born 1981–2000), and generation Z or centennials (PwC, 2019). Each generation has distinctive characteristics that can engender friction with those around them but also provide different ideas, experiences, and skills that can contribute to the family and the business. Most leaders of family firms anticipate that the next CEO in the company is likely to be a family member of the millennial generation, a group not only with a high level of education but also with a different orientation to work, as they generally plan to retire before they turn 50 years old (Calabrò & Valentino, 2019). The younger generations of family firms have been recently characterized as transformers (46%), administrators (26%), intrapreneurs (20%), and entrepreneurs (8%) (PwC, 2019). Transformers are those who aspire to lead a significant change in the family business by holding executive positions within five years. Administrators focus on maintaining the profitability and sustainability of the company in the long term, developing an administrative function. Intrapreneurs seek to establish their own company within the family business and will probably need to demonstrate their value in business management before presenting ideas for change. Finally, entrepreneurs seek to exit the family firm in order to build their own businesses. Unfortunately, the amount of academic research on how the younger generation perceives their participation within the family firm is practically nil. While Latin American youth might resemble younger generations elsewhere, this notion remains to be examined. The author's impression is that across most countries there is a fair amount of pessimism among youth about future opportunities. While democracy has been established in most countries and the military are in their barracks rather than in civilian roles, there is a general sense that corruption is endemic and that it is difficult to compete in a transparent and ethical way. For young people trying to break into the middle class and succeed in business, particularly within family firms, the widely held idea that corruption is a necessary evil to survive represents a major challenge for this coming generation. Interestingly, while most family firms in Latin America favor low-risk projects, adopt a cautious stance in decision-making, and avoid taking risks, which is a reasonable response to environmental threats, about half of them have introduced new lines of products or services and more than one-third have made dramatic changes in products or services in recent years. This might indicate that innovation is seen as essential by family firms to compete in this difficult environment. For young people, this represents an opportunity to make a difference as they are more likely to bring new ideas into the company as they are less wedded to doing things "the old fashion way."

On a world stage Calabrò and Valentino (2019) argue that young people working for family firms are concerned with a number of issues affecting the business such as digital transformation and technology, talent availability, taxes and regulations, as well as supply chain problems (Calabrò & Valentino, 2019). In Latin America, moreover, this next generation is also concerned with having a clearly defined purpose, achieving significant change and investing in new business ideas (PwC, 2019). This younger generation is generally aware of their limitations regarding levels of experience inside and outside the company (PwC, 2019). They feel generally ready to deal with the external threats and opportunities of disruptive change in the market (Deloitte, 2017). However, they perceive two important internal challenges: changing family relationships and leadership succession (Deloitte, 2017).

The Latin American region presents particular characteristics internal to the family firm and related to the context (Botero & Betancourt, 2016). On the one hand, family firms in this region tend to be young (led by the first or the second generation) and to keep a highly concentrated business ownership. On the other hand, the context in Latin America implies fragile and volatile economies as well as weak institutions and social inequality.

Power in these firms is concentrated at the top with the family maintaining a tight grip on that power (Vazquez et al., 2020) and business opportunities are chosen and pursued by a small family circle (Rodriguez, Matajira, Auletta, & Gonzalez, 2018), making it difficult to open opportunities for younger people entering the business.

While the main roles in family firms will be filled by members of the younger generations of these entrepreneurial families in the near future, 70% of current family business leaders worldwide did not have a succession plan in 2019 (Calabrò & Valentino, 2019), and we suspect that family firms in Latin America may fare even worse in this respect. The development of talent of the next generation of leaders of enterprising families in Latin America is very important, given their role in top decision positions. Besides the development of certain abilities, the degree of fit between the interests and work orientation of the next generation and the family firm will be critical to an effective succession process (Sharma et al., 2001).

Work Orientation of Next Generation in Family Firms

As the younger generations of members of enterprising families are likely to be involved in top decision-making, the transfer and/or development of business and entrepreneurial orientation to these generations is a critical element to achieve adequate performance and to guarantee the survival of the family business over time (Calabrò & Valentino, 2019). Achieving the satisfaction and commitment of capable and adequate successors in regard to relevant decision-making positions in the family firm have been indicated as important predictors of success and performance (Sharma et al., 2001; Sharma & Irving, 2005). Satisfaction, commitment, and effectiveness at work increase when work is a source of happiness and provides critical aspects of well-being such as positive emotions, engagement, relationships, meaning, and accomplishment (Seligman, 2011)

Not all individuals build the same type of bond with work or have the same work orientation. As mentioned before, most people see their work as a job, a career, or a calling (Wrzesniewski et al., 1997). A connection of an individual to his or her work as a job is configured on the basis of economic security, when work is considered a career it is associated to recognition and prestige, and if work is viewed as a career or vocation there is an identification with the activity as a source of meaning (Bellah, Madsen, Sullivan, Swidler, & Tipton, 1985). People have a work orientation of a job when it is only a means to provide material benefits that will then be used for enjoyment and satisfaction outside work. When work follows a career orientation, incumbents obtain not only monetary gains but also intrinsic satisfaction such as a feeling of achievements such as self-esteem and social standing by progressing in an organizational structure. Finally, when work is experienced as a calling or vocation it is inseparable of life, an end in itself, whose activity provides fulfillment and happiness. While a job is detached from the personal interests and a career subordinates personal to professional life, work experienced as a calling is fully aligned with an individual's personal interests, tastes, and passion, meaning that work is inseparable from life. Unlike employment and career, which are both mainly instrumental to extrinsic individual motives, work lived as a calling harmonizes personal and professional life as the person enjoys self-identification, meaningful relationships, satisfaction, and purpose at work. Positive psychology has made important contributions in the relationship between work and happiness and the work orientation toward a calling is associated with work as an experience capable of conferring orientation and meaning on life (Wrzesniewski et al., 1997).

According to the systemic view of the family business the individual, company, and family function as an integrated whole (Habbershon et al., 2003). Individual family members need to experience fulfillment in order for the family business system to be successful. This becomes particularly important during succession given that individual family members face the choice to remain in the company or go to work elsewhere. The work orientation of family members involved in succession at their family firms has been studied and four key distinctive motivations have been identified for members of the next generation to enter a succession process. These four elements include affective, normative, calculative, and imperative drivers (Sharma & Irving, 2005). The commitment of a member of the next generation is affective when it is based on the individual's emotional attachment and identification with the firm. This results in a strong alignment with the purpose and goals of the organization and an intense desire to contribute to the firm through involvement as eventual successor. The strong alignment and attachment experienced signalize that the member of the next generation can fulfill his individual aspirations in the family firm through an exchange and mutual benefit. Many characteristics of the affective commitment resemble the orientation to work as a calling or vocation.

The members of the younger generations are normatively committed to the firm in situations where the individuals have a strong feeling of obligation to be involved and to eventually succeed the older generation. Normative commitment by the next generation is mostly based in an intention to keep positive relationships with other family members. Several aspects of work as a career such as complying with an organizational advancement program can be associated with normative commitment.

The calculative commitment of the next generation is mostly transactional and aimed at avoiding the expected cost of not participating in the organization. In this case, the younger generation perceives that the participation in the family firm is the best of several acceptable alternatives available. Similar to the calculative commitment in regard to its transactional nature, the imperative commitment is experienced by the next generations when involvement in the family firm is considered as the only acceptable employment alternative. The imperative commitment is therefore a response to a perceived lack of attractive alternative employment opportunities. Calculative and imperative commitments can be mostly associated to the orientation to work as employment not only as they mainly imply a transaction but also to some aspects of the work considered as a career.

The affective commitment by a family member of the next generation in regard to the involvement in the family firm is related to increased effort, stronger intentions of a long-term career, as well as enhanced alignment and intentions to contribute to the organization's goals (Sharma & Irving, 2005). This affective commitment, very related to most of the aspects of the conception of work as calling, is expected to contribute not only to the wellbeing and happiness of the family member working in the family firm but also to his work performance.

The Calling of the Family Firm for the Next Generations

For the family firm fostering the involvement of the next generations of family members, as well as for the younger generations that consider whether or not to join the family firm in the future, the affective commitment and calling orientation to work in the family firm are predispositions that increase the chances of success.

Four features have been argued as critical in order to experience work as a call: freedom, belonging, competence, and relevance (Rodríguez, 2016). The freedom requirement implies that the individual is inclined or identified with a specific occupation. The importance of belonging refers to the positioning and integration within a group and/or community. Competence is critical as the individual needs to feel gifted and capable of a good performance. Finally, the need for relevance means realizing that the task performed has a positive effect and is important to the whole.

The requirement of freedom to perceive work as calling has some specificities within the context of family firms. Children and young generations of enterprising families have the potential to achieve leadership positions (Schröder, Schmitt-Rodermund, & Arnaud, 2011). The possibility to participate in the family firm can be not only a great opportunity but also a burden for the members of the young generations. Individual interests, aspirations, and abilities, as well as interpersonal relationships, experiences, and group expectations can influence the positive or negative perception of the chance of involvement in the family firm. That is, individual family members may feel that they don't have the discretion to decline this opportunity. This places them in a situation where they are reluctant to join the family firm but feel that they have to. As a result, they may have a negative attitude when joining the family firm. This is a problem that is common in Latin America as good employment opportunities are rather limited to joining the family firm by young family members may not be much of a choice. On the other hand, there is strong identification of family members with the family firm, which is particularly true in Latin America, and this can be a source of deep emotional satisfaction for young family entrants.

The need for belonging also acquires specific characteristics in regard to the calling to work in the family firm. Children and young family members may feel included or excluded of the extended family and the family firm. Those who feel that the family and the family firm are very important parts of their self will most probably grow a stronger intention to belong and to contribute to the group and to the business (Schröder et al., 2011). Moreover, the family firm may be the place where several socioemotional needs of the family members such as identification, emotional attachment, social ties, and others are fulfilled (Berrone et al., 2012).

Psychologists have long argued that human beings have an innate need for competence, reflected in the ability to control outcomes and to achieve mastery related to certain activity (Reis, Sheldon, Gable, Roscoe, & Ryan, 2000); this is something that is also influenced by the context of the family firm. While usually the next generations enter the family firm not because selection but due to kinship, and even though enterprising families value trust and commitment to the family as an important characteristic of is leaders, young family members need to develop and exercise its competence and to feel competent for the work to exert a calling. Therefore, the family has to provide opportunities for the development and the exercise of competences. Many enterprising families not only invest heavily in education of young family members but also favor early work experiences in the family firm as well experience outside the family firm.

For work to be perceived as a calling, it needs to provide purpose and meaningful interpersonal relationships. The enterprising families and the family firm provide many opportunities for the younger generations to experience relevance. The next generations observe and perceive the meaning that work has for the elders, and therefore the older generations serve as models to experience relevant work. Moreover, family firms have been found to be especially socially responsible (Berrone, Cruz, Gomez-Mejía, & Larraza-Kintana, 2010), and the next generation is also likely to perceive the need for the family firm to continue along similar lines.

The next generation of leaders of family firms will considerably influence the economic and social contributions of these very relevant and prevalent organizational forms in Latin America. Therefore, their ability and willingness to participate in the top decision-making positions of family firms and to engage in socially responsible behaviors are important factors that may contribute to the welfare of the region. Hence as the orientation to work will not only determine individual outcomes of the younger generations of enterprising families but will also affect their families, their firms, and their communities, it is very important to develop their "calling."

Developing the Calling Orientation to Work in the Family Firm in Latin America

Entrepreneurial families have incentives to foster in their younger generations the calling orientation to work in the family firm. A capable successor who perceives a calling for getting involved in the family firm will increase not only his individual happiness but also the probability of business success. To nurture the calling orientation to work in the family firm, attention must be paid to the affective commitment of the next generation, to the critical conditions necessary to experience work as a call, and to succession planning.

Affective commitment by young family members in Latin America can be promoted through developing a desire to participate in the family firm, which again is the dominant organizational form in the region. This underlying mindset is experienced when individuals perceive the alignment between the self-identity and that of an organization on the one hand, and the interests and professional opportunities available in the organization on the other hand (Sharma & Irving, 2005). Identity alignment occurs when aspects of the identity, values, and interests of the individual are similar to those of the organization, originating a feeling of belonging. When there is identity alignment, the perception of attractive professional opportunities in the family firm generates a strong motivation for the next generation to pursue involvement and to dedicate strong efforts in order to contribute to the organization. One of the unique characteristics of Latin American family firms is a strong sense of connection of the family identity to the business identity and an inclination of the young generations to contribute to the family and to the firm (Feliu Costa, 2018). The Latin American culture with its strong Catholic roots can help enhance this identity of individual family members with the firm. Conversely, if the sense of identity and professional interests of the next generations are not aligned with their family firms, or if there is a stronger alignment with other organizations or a perception of lack of opportunities within the family firm, their levels of affective commitment are expected to be low. This may occur in Latin America as a result of migration of young people to more developed countries (particularly the ones with higher levels of education) or to a feeling that there are better ways to succeed in life such as entering the civil service, the military, or politics.

Calls can also be promoted if some critical job characteristics are developed. These characteristics are freedom of choice, sense of belonging, development, and application of own capacities, as well as the feeling of relevance, and these characteristics have some particularities when it comes to family firms (Schröder et al., 2011). The possibility of participating in the family business can be a burden or an opportunity depending on individual interests, aspirations, and abilities, as well as interpersonal relationships, experiences, and group expectations. Freedom of choice in the family business is the voluntary option to work or not in the family business, with fair chances of aspiring to leadership positions. Unfortunately, some characteristics of many Latin American enterprising families such as strong patriarchal beliefs, tendency to keep tight control, difficulties to deal with disagreement, and different points of view, as well as an excessive tendency to only accept consensus (Feliu Costa, 2018) may cause that the younger generations see work in the family firm as an obligation. If a high proportion of young people in Latin America join the family firm because they think they have to rather than through a voluntary choice this may reduce the commitment to see the firm succeed or may use the firm as a source of income rather than a place deserving of their full dedication.

The sense of belonging to the family business is associated with the feelings of inclusion or exclusion in the extended family and the family business. The intention to belong and contribute to the group and the business will be stronger if the members of the next generation feel that their family and family firm are very important parts of themselves. Involvement of multiple generations of a family in a business is not only challenging but also a source of advantages (Miller & Le Breton-Miller, 2006, p. 83). The next generation of entrepreneurial families feel they have the tools and skills to adapt and respond to the digital age, to professionalize management, and to attract talent (Deloitte, 2017). Combining the advantages of the next generations with the experience of the previous generations is challenging and involves recognizing the best traits of each generation (PwC, 2019). In this respect, an important challenge for Latin American family firms is to incorporate generational diversity and women to the top decision-making positions such as the Board of Directors, as the intergenerational overlap as well as female presence in these bodies is rather low (Carrera et al., 2019). The patriarchal nature of Latin American culture makes overcoming this traditional practice within family firms rather difficult.

The development and application of the own capacities in the family business are favored by opportunities for early work experiences inside and outside the family business. The young family members must develop and exercise competence as well as feel competent for the tasks involved in order the work to exert a calling. In Latin America, enterprising families tend to give high importance to the education of the younger generations, what includes not only academic education in top schools but also business knowledge and incentives to entrepreneurial projects (Feliu Costa, 2018). However, a common problem, as noted earlier, is in Latin America those who have received strong educational credentials and are well-trained in academic institutions (often abroad for the most prosperous families) may be reluctant to come back and work for the family firm. They might do it as an obligation but may not be fully committed to see the firm succeed.

Finally, the next generations will most likely experience the feeling of relevance in regard to the meaning that work has for previous generations and also to evidence of the social responsibility of their families and companies. In Latin America, enterprising families are usually socially responsible as an expression of their values and religious beliefs as well as a way to respond to an environment of social and economic inequality (Feliu Costa, 2018). Undoubtedly, exhibiting social responsibility is also a way for family firms in Latin America to gain legitimacy in a risky institutional environment and this may help reduce some of the business risks that the firm could face.

Last but not least, early, and effective succession planning is very important in promoting a call to future generations to work in the family business. For the succession plan to be successful, the intentions of parents and the willingness and ability of eventual successful are both very important. A strong preference to have a successor from the own offspring as well as adequate preparation by parents increases the likelihood of developing succession intentions in the family firm by the younger generations, compared to starting a new business or working as employee elsewhere (Schröder et al., 2011). This shows that succession is a process that starts very early, and implies that the way that everything related to the family firm is experienced and communicated by the parents to their children, intentionally or unintentionally, will shape the interest, intentions, and work orientation of the younger generations in regard to an eventual position in the family firm. More than half of leaders of family firms do not have a retirement plan (Calabrò & Valentino, 2019). Moreover, the high sense of respect to the elders as well as a the patriarchal authority and centralized decision-making that are usually observed in Latin American family firms are many times obstacles as any comment or intention to plan succession could be considered as a provocation to the leading authority (Feliu Costa, 2018). In many

Latin American family firms, it may also be seen as an indiscretion or even an expression of greed or disloyalty for a younger family member to show interest in taking on a leadership role.

While we have seen that freedom of choice is critical for the next generation of family members to experience the calling orientation to work in the family firm, enterprising families, who want to nurture this calling must consider the importance of developing affective commitment, to create and maintain some critical conditions necessary to experience work as a call, as well as to plan and manage succession from the early stages.

Conclusion

In the Latin American context, family members have significant involvement in leading positions of ownership, boards of directors, and top management of family enterprises. This strong family involvement also anticipates that the younger generations of enterprising families such as "millennials" and "centennials" will be occupying leading positions in years to come. These generations will have to run the business and face the external challenges specific to the region, such as fragile and volatile economies, widespread corruption, weak institutions, and social inequality. Moreover, while dealing with the business and its context, and in order for the system of the family firm to be successful, they will also have to keep family cohesion in the midst of intense economic pressure and to provide individual fulfillment of the new family generation when asked to join the family firm. The interest, motivation, preparation, and effort required for this next generation to achieve these multiple and diverse outcomes at individual, group, and organizational levels, will be influenced by the external environment. Motivation, effort, and satisfaction of the younger generations to work in the family firm will be lower if they feel that the environment in Latin America will make it difficult for the family firm to survive and prosper. Conversely, if the members of the next generation of enterprising families in Latin America feel a calling to work in the family firm, they will fully enjoy and commit to the task, with the purpose to contribute to the group, the organization and the relevant community. This will most likely happen if these next generation members feel that working in the family firm is connected to their interests and passion, and if they can find identity, meaningful relationships, satisfaction, and purpose at work.

Because family values are deeply ingrained in Latin America and respect for elders is expected among the youth this should facilitate the role modeling by the elders to serve as a guide for incoming generations. Hence this calling for youth to work in the family firm is mostly the responsibility of the parents and older generations, as they serve as role models and provide the context in which the younger generations explore and discover their interests and abilities. Open conversations about the family firm, invitations to know and to get involved in the business early (even as conducting specific projects or to participate in summer jobs or internships), transfer of values, capabilities, and expectations, are all activities that parents need to undertake in the early life of the young generations. While this may be true in many regions of the world, it is especially true in Latin America given the environmental turbulence surrounding family firms and the critical role of the family as an institution within the cultural milieu. Under the tutelage of elders, in Latin America positive and constructive intergenerational dynamics within the enterprising family and a well-designed and implemented succession process are also crucial contributors for the effective arrival of the next generation to top positions of the family firm. An active and systematic fostering by elders for their younger generations to find their calling to work in the family firm will grow the chances of intentions for succession, increase commitment and effort, and develop higher alignment to the family legacy and vision.

References

Basco, R. 2015. Family business and regional development—A theoretical model of regional familiness. *Journal of Family Business Strategy*, 6(4): 259–271.

Bellah, R. N., Madsen, R., Sullivan, W. M., Swidler, A., & Tipton, S. M. 1985. *Habits of the heart*. Berkeley, CA: University of California Press.

Berrone, P., Cruz, C., & Gomez Mejía, L. R. 2012. Socioemotional wealth in family firms: Theoretical dimensions, assessment approaches, and agenda for future research. *Family Business Review*, 25(3): 258–279.

Berrone, P., Cruz, C., Gomez-Mejia, L. R., & Larraza-Kintana, M. 2010. Socioemotional wealth and corporate responses to institutional pressures: Do family-controlled firms pollute less? *Administrative Science Quarterly*, 55(1): 82–113.

Botero, I. C., & Betancourt, G. G. 2016. Contextual factors that affect selection and use of governance structures in Latin American family enterprises. In *The Routledge companion to family business* (pp. 579–596). Abingdon: Routledge.

Calabrò, A., & Valentino, A. 2019. *STEP 2019 Global family business survey*, France.

Carrera, A., Vazquez, P., & Cornejo, M. 2019. ¿Cómo se gobiernan las mayores empresas de Contol Familiar de América Latina? *Harvard Deusto Business Review*, 285: 62–69.

Deloitte. 2017. *Next generation family businesses leading a family business in a disruptive environment*. Machelen: Deloittte University EMEA CVBA.

Duran, P., van Essen, M., Heugens, P. P., Kostova, T., & Peng, M. W. 2019. The impact of institutions on the competitive advantage of publicly listed family firms in emerging markets. *Global Strategy Journal*, 9(2): 243–274.

Faccio, M., & Lang, L. H. 2002. The ultimate ownership of Western European corporations. *Journal of Financial Economics*, 65(3): 365–395.

Feliu Costa, N. 2018. Latin American family businesses and their role as new global competitors. In C. G. Müller, I. C. Botero, A. D. Cruz, & R. Subramanian (Eds.), *Family firms in Latin America* (pp. 8–13). New York: Routledge.

Gómez-Mejía, L., Haynes, K., Núñez-Nickel, M., Jacobson, K., & Moyano-Fuentes, J. 2007. Socioemotional wealth and business risks in family-controlled firms: Evidence from Spanish olive oil mills. *Administrative Science Quarterly*, 52(1): 106–137.

Habbershon, T. G., Williams, M., & MacMillan, I. C. 2003. A unified systems perspective of family firm performance. *Journal of Business Venturing*, 18(4): 451–465.

IFERA. 2003. Family businesses dominate: International Family Enterprise Research Academy (IFERA). *Family Business Review*, 16(4): 235–240.

Lansberg, I., & Perrow, E. 1991. Understanding and working with leading family businesses in Latin America. *Family Business Review*, 4(2): 127–147.

La Porta, R., Lopez-de-Silanes, F., & Shleifer, A. 1999. Corporate ownership around the world. *The Journal of Finance*, 54(2): 471–517.

Miller, D., & Le Breton-Miller, I. 2006. Family governance and firm performance: Agency, stewardship, and capabilities. *Family Business Review*, 19(1): 73–87.

Nordqvist, M., Sharma, P., & Chirico, F. 2014. Family firm heterogeneity and governance: A configuration approach. *Journal of Small Business Management*, 52(2): 192–209.

Perkins, G. 2017. *Empresas Familiares. Dirigiendo lo Nuestro*. Buenos Aires: Temas.

PwC. 2019. *PwC's global NextGen survey 2019*.

Reis, H. T., Sheldon, K. M., Gable, S. L., Roscoe, J., & Ryan, R. M. 2000. Daily well-being: The role of autonomy, competence, and relatedness. *Personality and Social Psychology Bulletin*, 26(4): 419–435.

Rodríguez, O. 2016. *Calling: el trabajo como vocación en la Psicología Positiva*. Pamplona: Universidad de Navarra.

Rodriguez, Y., Matajira, L., Auletta, N., & Gonzalez, A. 2018. *Transgenerational entrepreneurship practices in family firms: Perspectives of Latin America (STEP Survey)*.

Schröder, E., Schmitt-Rodermund, E., & Arnaud, N. 2011. Career choice intentions of adolescents with a family business background. *Family Business Review*, 24(4): 305–321.

Seligman, M. E. 2011. *Flourish: A visionary new understanding of happiness and wellbeing*. New York: Free Press.

Sharma, P., Chrisman, J. J., Pablo, A. L., & Chua, J. H. 2001. Determinants of initial satisfaction with the succession process in family firms: A conceptual model. *Entrepreneurship Theory and Practice*, 25(3): 17–36.

Sharma, P., & Irving, P. G. 2005. Four bases of family business successor commitment: Antecedents and consequences. *Entrepreneurship Theory and Practice*, 29(1): 13–33.

Vassolo, R. S., De Castro, J. O., & Gomez-Mejia, L. R. 2011. Managing in Latin America: Common issues and a research agenda. *The Academy of Management Perspectives*, 25(4): 22–36.

Vázquez, P. 2017. *SEW & CSP: Do family controlled firms employ larger work-forces? Evidence from the largest Latin American firms*. Atlanta: Academy of Management.

Vazquez, P., Carrera, A., & Cornejo, M. 2020. Corporate governance in the largest family firms in Latin America. *Cross Cultural & Strategic Management*, 27(2): 137–163.

Vazquez, P., & Rocha, H. 2018. On the goals of family firms: A review and integration. *Journal of Family Business Strategy*, 9(2): 94–106.

Wrzesniewski, A., McCauley, C., Rozin, P., & Schwartz, B. 1997. Jobs, careers, and callings: People's relations to their work. *Journal of Research in Personality*, 31(1): 21–33.

6 How Socially Responsible HRM Should Be Understood in Latin America

Anabella Davila

The fundamentals of socially responsible human resource management (SRHRM) relate to developing employees' attitudes and support to the organization's CSR actions and promoting employee wellbeing and satisfaction at work (Orlitzky & Swanson, 2006; Stahl, Brewster, Collings, & Hajro, 2020). However, there is a need to understand what CSR means for a given organization because it would determine the CSR orientation. Organization-centered CSR favors performance and global standardization of CSR actions aligned to the corporate principles and business scope (Bondy & Starkey, 2014). In contrast, understanding what CSR means for society requires analyzing the business–society social contract. This perspective is particular to developing countries and integrates the contextual characteristics into the CSR actions and strategies, making CSR relevant (Bondy & Starkey, 2014; Jamali & Karam, 2018). In this vein, SRHRM requires a broader view of CSR beyond employees' behaviors and attitudes toward CSR activities, including their embeddedness within the larger context.

This chapter introduces the concept of SRHRM as it emerges in the Latin American socioeconomic context. The chapter presents a comparative analysis of the Latin American labor market contexts in which HRM systems operate through three perspectives: the human capital paradigm, the institutional voids framework, and the stakeholder perspective.

Based on the contextual challenges of HRM in the region, this chapter suggests that SRHRM comprises a "developer" of human capital and the appropriate supporting social infrastructure. Contextual challenges influence HRM to respond to "promoting" necessary labor market effectiveness, which implies strengthening labor institutions. Finally, the HRM models identified in the Latin American region include all stakeholders involved in or affected by a given employment relationship. Under this perspective, companies grant HRM the responsibility of being a "provider" for human development (e.g., education, health, and living standards).

The organization of the chapter is as follows. The first section briefly introduces the mainstream approaches to SRHRM and the challenges in the Latin American region. The second section reviews the human capital paradigm and the role of SRHRM to enhance the appropriate social infrastructure. The third section addresses the institutional voids that emerged because of the opening of the Latin American economies and the role that SRHRM adopts to minimize labor markets' inefficiencies. The fourth section presents the SRHRM role derived from the stakeholder perspective. The chapter ends with final remarks on how SRHRM should be understood in Latin America.

Socially Responsible Human Resource Management

The mainstream literature on SRHRM seeks to align HRM practices to develop socially responsible employees' behaviors and attitudes to achieve the organization's CSR objectives (Orlitzky & Swanson, 2006; Stahl et al., 2020). Scholars argue that SRHRM can develop employee commitment and engagement toward the organization's CSR objectives and strategy through practices such as values-based recruitment and selection, induction training, employee development, talent management, and performance management and incentive systems (Stahl et al., 2020). Similarly, CSR can enhance HRM through activities such as creating an employer brand, attracting talent, acknowledge unbiased selection procedures, how to interpret decent work principles, aligning rewarding systems to the achievements of the CSR objectives, and developing the spirit of volunteerism among the employees (Stahl et al., 2020). However, in both views of the HRM-CSR integration, CSR needs to be central to the business; otherwise, the two areas would benefit little from each other.

This mainstream of the SRHRM literature emphasizes HRM practices' alignment to the organization's CSR objectives and strategies that mainly benefit external stakeholders—e.g., community members, children of school age, or vulnerable groups—and how they impact the organization. Although this framing is an essential component of the CSR organizational dimension, its narrow approach provides partial explanations for the advancement of SRHRM. However, when addressing this issue, the literature proposes that CSR initiatives should focus on employees' development and personal needs, mostly referring to job-related issues such as wellbeing, job security, or organizational justice. In other words, the concern in this stream is how the organization treats its employees (Stahl et al., 2020). Further, when including the organization's international operations, the CSR literature emphasizes compliance with local labor laws and regulations (Shen, 2011). Thus, research continues addressing how an employee-centered CSR approach can benefit the organization with limited understanding of the employee human development or societal advancement.

While the HRM-CSR conceptual integration expands, there is an opportunity to advance SRHRM knowledge by studying organizations that face unique societal challenges. Such is the case of organizations operating in Latin America, a region with distinctive development characteristics. In Latin America, the social infrastructure for human development (i.e., health, education, and living standards) tends to be precarious. Governments either do not have the resources to provide it or have lost their capacity to build the appropriate conditions for an acceptable living standard (Davila, 2019). In such circumstances, local communities develop high expectations that business organizations would invest in building such social infrastructure (Contreras, 2004; Davila, 2019; Gifford & Kestler, 2008). The expectations reach HRM with demands for bridging between the organization and the communities' social development via employment conditions. Thus, SRHRM in Latin America starts by being sensitive to the employees' and communities' expectations about the impact of work on individuals' and communities' quality of life. In other words, SRHRM needs to discern the specific context to understand better the institutional arrangement of interrelationships among the employees, their families, and the community.

The chapter now turns to identify the Latin American region's socioeconomic conditions, the challenges in the realm of SRHRM, and the role SRHRM adopts to encounter those challenges.

The Human Capital Paradigm

The literature on human capital stresses that the construct initially sought to measure the individuals' market value of their knowledge, skills, abilities, and other characteristics (KSAO) (Becker, 2009). However, individuals' KSAO contribution to the organization translates into its value for the strategic objectives and performance (Nyberg & Wright, 2015). In this view, organizations seek individuals to become a source of competitive advantage. Thus, the HR area's role is to design competitive HRM practices to attract and retain the right people. Moreover, organizations need to create competitive organizational systems to facilitate individuals' contributions to what Lawler (2009) called the HC-centric organization.

To design competitive HRM systems in Latin America, organizations should first review the labor market competitiveness indicators and the countries' classification in global indexes. Let us look at the data related to the talent competitiveness in Latin America. Although several comparative studies and technical reports describe the countries' economic and labor profile in the region, the Global Competitiveness Report, published by the World Economic Forum (WEF), provides essential data to design competitive HRM practices.

The 2019 Global Competitiveness Index (GCI) 4.0 developed a framework within the context of the Fourth Industrial Revolution to rank the countries around the globe. It maps the factors and attributes that drive productivity, growth, and human development. According to a group of institutions, policies, and factors that determine productivity, the report defines a country's competitiveness. It covers 141 economies, accounting for 99% of its global domestic product. The GCI 4.0 includes 103 indicators provided by international organizations and the WEF's Executive Opinion Survey that measures the country's performance on a 0–100 scale. Thus, nations can follow their progress over time. The GCI 4.0 organizes the indicators into 12 drivers of productivity or "pillars": Institutions, Infrastructure, ICT adoption, macroeconomic stability, Health, Skills, Product market, Labor market, Financial system, Market size, Business dynamism, and innovation capability.

Overall, the report highlights the urgent need to increase competitiveness and improve productivity and growth to globally impact living standards. In the global index, Chile (33rd) scores as the most competitive Latin American economy because of its stable macroeconomic context. Then comes Mexico (48th), Uruguay (54th), and Colombia (57th). Brazil ranges low (71st) while Venezuela ranges the most down economy of the region (133rd). Table 6.1 provides the Competitiveness Index 4.0 scores of the Latin American countries.

Table 6.1 Latin American Competitiveness Index 4.0

Rank 141	Country	Value (0–100)
33	Chile	70.5
48	Mexico	64.9
54	Uruguay	63.5
57	Colombia	62.7
62	Costa Rica	62.0
65	Peru	61.7
66	Panama	61.6
71	Brazil	60.9
83	Argentina	57.2
90	Ecuador	55.7
97	Paraguay	53.6
98	Guatemala	53.5
101	Honduras	52.6
103	El Salvador	52.6
107	Bolivia	51.8
109	Nicaragua	51.5
133	Venezuela	41.8

Source: Created by the author based on the World Economic Forum: Global Competitiveness Report 2019. Accessed June 15, 2020, through http://reports.weforum.org/global-competitiveness-report-2019/competitiveness-rankings/

Although all pillars affect in a way or another organizations' HRM systems, Pillar 5, related to health, and Pillar 6, related to skills, offer evidence on how SRHRM can build the appropriate supporting social infrastructure to develop human capital in current and future employees. See Table 6.2 for the scores of the Latin American countries on Pillars 5 and 6.

Among the Latin American countries, Colombia scores the highest in Pillar 5 with 95/100 and Bolivia the lowest—73.7/100. Pillar 5 measures the healthy life expectancy defined as the number of years a newborn can expect to live in good health. This measurement considers the mortality and disability of the population in each country. Organizations must analyze the health services systems in countries with poor health because of the affectations on productivity. Moreover, deficient health services require a business to invest in the provision of health services. The following examples illustrate how Latin American companies build the social infrastructure to provide health services to the employees, their families, and relevant members of the community.

Table 6.2 Pillars 5 and 6 for Latin American Countries

Human Capital			Pillar 5 Health			Pillar 6 Skills		
Rank (141)	Country	Human Capital (0–100)	Rank (141)	Country	Health (0–100)	Rank (141)	Country	Skills (0–100)
33	Costa Rica	81.1	16	Colombia	95.0	31	Argentina	72.3
34	Chile	79.7	19	Peru	94.6	47	Chile	69.8
39	Argentina	78.0	25	Costa Rica	93.2	51	Costa Rica	69.0
42	Colombia	77.7	32	Panama	92.0	60	Uruguay	66.8
44	Peru	77.4	35	Nicaragua	90.0	68	Venezuela	63.7
52	Uruguay	75.9	37	Chile	89.7	76	Ecuador	61.4
56	Panama	75.2	50	Ecuador	85.0	80	Colombia	60.5
65	Ecuador	73.2	51	Uruguay	85.0	81	Peru	60.2
68	Venezuela	72.8	53	Argentina	83.8	88	Panama	58.5
76	Mexico	70.1	60	Mexico	82.0	89	Mexico	58.3
85	Nicaragua	68.4	61	Venezuela	81.9	91	Bolivia	57.9
86	Brazil	67.9	63	Paraguay	81.4	96	Brazil	56.4
92	Paraguay	66.1	75	Brazil	79.4	103	Guatemala	51.4
94	Bolivia	65.8	77	El Salvador	78.1	106	Paraguay	50.8
97	Honduras	63.7	80	Honduras	77.8	108	Honduras	49.5
98	El Salvador	63.3	88	Guatemala	74.0	112	El Salvador	48.4
99	Guatemala	62.7	89	Bolivia	73.7	116	Nicaragua	46.8

Source: Created by the author based on the World Economic Forum (2019). The Global Competitiveness Report 2019. Accessed June 3, 2020, through https://www.weforum.org/reports/how-to-end-a-decade-of-lost-productivity-growth

Grupo Alfa (Mexican-Diversified Conglomerate) reports evidence of investments in health services for the employees and their families and community members. The company offers nutrition coaching services, vaccination campaigns, and annual check-ups for all the employees. In 1977, the company inaugurated the Nova Health Clinic for the employees and their families. Today, Nova is a general hospital, and Ternium Mexico (Argentinean-Steel) manages it and in 2017 invested 5.8 million dollars for its infrastructure upgrading.

At the time of writing this chapter, the entire world is suffering from the pandemic COVID-19. Latin America is struggling with the limited capacity of the health systems to respond to the crisis. Business organizations are implementing various health initiatives to prevent transmission and alleviate the shortage of equipment in health institutions. However, some organizations go further in their actions. At the end of March 2020, Ternium Argentina provided more than 270 tons of steel to fabricate modular hospitals to respond to the COVID-19 crisis (CEPAL, 2020).

Moreover, in April 2020, Ternium Mexico invested 30 million Mexican pesos in a community hospital near its leading manufacturing site in Monterrey's northern city. The company built a hospital in 12 days, anticipating the pandemic's outbreak at no cost to the state or users. Máximo Vedoya, President of Ternium Global, announced the community hospital's investment, given the possible public and private hospitals' possible saturation to serve patients infected with COVID-19 (González, 2020).

Pillar 6 assesses the workforce's general level of skills and the quantity and quality of education reported by the World Bank and evaluated by business leaders. The average rating in this pillar substantiates the competitiveness of factors such as the secondary and tertiary education enrollment rate, quality of the education systems, quality of math and science education, internet access in schools, local availability of specialized training services, and staff training. This last item referred to the extent to which companies invested in training and employee development. Quality factors include developing digital literacy, interpersonal skills, and the ability to think critically and creatively.

The report stresses that investments in skills development and other factors are inadequate for improving productivity in the current and future workforce for all economies. The analysis proposes that technological and innovation advancements need to occur through human capital investments. Workers require the right skills to adapt to the technology life cycles. Improving talent adaptability is also another challenge captured by Pillar 6 on Skills. Workers need high-level skills to be able to perform complex tasks and adapt rapidly to changing business models. Such is the case of the manufacturing movement of industry 4.0 based on the advancements of digitalization. In this Pillar, Argentina scored the highest among the Latin American countries with 72.3/100, and Nicaragua the lowest—46.8/100. In general, Latin American countries score a disperse assessment along the skills' sub-criteria that point to the need to improve workers' skills beyond in-house training programs.

Organizations require pools of high-skilled workers to make human capital a source of competitive advantage. In this vein, organizations make serious efforts to develop human capital in their current and future employees throughout the region. In 2016, Ternium Mexico (Argentinean-Steel) invested US$30 million in building the Roberto Rocca Technical School in Monterrey in Northern Mexico. The vocational school has 374 students, and 99% of them have a particular type of scholarship. Although Ternium Mexico provides a high percentage of the scholarships, other major companies also contribute to the student fund—e.g., Kia Motors, Vydmsa, Denso, Festo, Grupo Alfa, and its subsidiaries. The purpose of the school is to provide high academic education to the youth of the community. The educational model consists of integrating the students with the industry and the use of cutting-edge technology. A market study on vocational schools shows a deficit of 10,000–15,000 technicians in the area when Ternium announced the investment in the educational initiative (Flores, 2015).

Orbia Group (Mexican, [formely Mexichen]—Diversified Conglomerate) manufactures PVC piping in the Guachené plant in the Industrial and Commercial Park of Cauca, the poorest regions of Colombia and that is continuously affected by local violence. The zone is surrounded by small towns, inhabited mainly by communities living in extreme poverty, who have no potable water services, and have a deficient education level. In 2009, Orbia committed to working with natives of the region, investing in intensive training programs to develop the required production process skills to obtain positive financial and productivity indicators. The company reported that employees from the area comprise 82% of the payroll, and some are in leadership positions such as supervisors and process engineers (Mexichen, 2009).

The competitiveness indicators related to human capital development clearly show how the region presents macro-structural challenges in health and education to enhance business competitiveness. The selected examples in this section illustrate the premise that SRHRM in the area includes developing human capital by investing in supporting social infrastructure in health and education. Moreover, the developer role falls into the responsibility of SRHRM because it assures jobs to the community members that already benefit from the social infrastructure.

The Institutional Voids Framework

The institutional voids' framework's main argument is that emerging markets have weak institutions that fail to protect businesses or lack market intermediaries that prevent them from functioning effectively (Khanna & Palepu, 2010). Such market deficiencies give rise to institutional voids. Then, informal mechanisms arise, and organizations and individuals use them to fulfill those gaps or roles.

Multinational corporations (MNCs) operating in emerging markets often encounter market failures, poor-quality legal and regulatory institutions, and lack of reliable trading partners (Khanna & Palepu, 1997). MNCs discover that they must perform essential institutional functions themselves (Khanna & Palepu, 2010).

In addition to Khanna and Palepu's (2010) argument that MNCs need to perform some vital institutional functions themselves, research provides evidence on how local firms compensate for institutional voids in the realm of labor market effectiveness. A recent study on firms from Sub-Saharan Africa that have human capital voids (the absence of employees with the right skills or with any skill) shows that firms used external mechanisms such as alliances with foreign partners to acquire ready-to-use knowledge. The partnership proved to reduce the negative effect of the lack of human capital on firm performance. The study also analyzed internal mechanisms such as local firms investing in research and development, but this mechanism increased the negative effect of human capital void on firm performance (Wang & Cuervo-Cazurra, 2017). Thus, to prevent the detriment of the company's performance due to the lack of human capital skills in labor markets of underdeveloped countries, managers require to select mechanisms that limit the negative impact, and compensate for the absence of their personnel's skills (Wang & Cuervo-Cazurra, 2017).

In Latin America, the primary form of business organization is that of a business group. A business group is a set of "legally separate firms bound together in persistent formal and/or informal ways" (Granovetter, 2005; p. 429). The main argument behind the structure of a business group in the region is that due to the lack of efficient market institutions, such structure provides internal mechanisms that help companies compensate for institutional voids (Khanna & Rivkin, 2001). Also, business groups respond to entrepreneurs, families, and alliances' unique skills and abilities to mobilize resources within the business group or among networks of other business groups (Granovetter, 2005). In this vein, research shows that in Latin America, group-affiliated firms are more innovative than stand-alone firms because they have access to internal financial resources and workers with the right training. Thus, business groups efficiently allocate labor resources internally to enhance innovation (Castellacci, 2015).

The institutional voids framework also includes the challenges derived from labor market inefficiencies in emerging economies. For example, there are questions regarding the educational institutions and their effectiveness in developing human capital or offering quality certifications (Khanna & Palepu, 2010). Another set of questions is related to labor regulations' efficacy and the protection of the contractual employment relationship and the workers' rights. More questions arise on issues linked to the country's education on technical and managerial training and business environment. For example, there are questions regarding English language qualification for business, societal, and cultural support for job mobility, pay-for-performance culture versus seniority, enforcement of employment contracts to protect confidential information, labor unions power use to protect the workers or for political advancement, labor rights, stock options compensation schemes, regulations for restructuring, downsizing or closing businesses, and international reputation (Khanna & Palepu, 2010).

Regarding labor regulations in Latin America, they are rigid and costly because of the high restrictions on workers' hiring and dismissal. The consequences of these restrictions are that firms avoid downsizing during cyclical downturns and limit hiring high-skill workers during upswings. For workers, legal rigidity makes them afraid of losing their severance pay and avoid changing jobs that require new skills (Phillips, Mehrez, & Moissinac, 2006).

Pillar 8 of the GCI 4.0 assesses labor market competitiveness. In the era of globalization and digitalization, labor market competitiveness indicators measure the protection that governments offer to workers rather than jobs. This approach has to do with security in times of unemployment, flexible contractual arrangements, life-long learning, and protection for workers' rights. That is, there is a need to focus on workers' demands for security. Chile scores the highest points in this Pillar with 62.8 out of 100, and Bolivia the lowest with 46.1 out of 100. The sub-criteria measuring competitiveness relates to job flexibility and meritocracy, and incentivization.

Once more, Latin American countries score disperse in several of the labor market competitiveness indicators' sub-criteria. It seems that some criteria might relate to the organization's culture and HRM philosophy and policies. Such is the case of issues related to meritocracy and incentivization. However, the other indicators relate more to national and local labor laws and regulations. In this vein, scholars stress that governments in emerging markets do not have the state capacity to enforce international labor standards successfully (Berliner, Greenleaf, Lake, & Noveck, 2015). Thus, if governmental institutions are incapable of building effective labor market structures through legislation, other societal actors with legitimate power could promote the appropriate conditions to ensure workers' well-being beyond regulations. In Latin America, workers largely depend on companies' decisions for job protection, salary, and benefits that provide workers and their family's welfare, and workers' participation in favorable labor relations (Davila & Elvira, 2018).

Then, the question is, how can SRHRM compensate for the institutional voids of local labor markets in Latin America? The contextual challenges require that SRHRM respond to promoting the appropriate labor infrastructure for workers and their family's wellbeing, which implies strengthening labor institutions. Thus, SRHRM's promoter role is best performed when social arrangements consist of local, state, and federal agents, including national and multinational firms in improving labor market effectiveness. The following example illustrates how the company led an initiative to compensate for educational deficiencies in the workforce through societal actors' network.

ARAUCO's (Chilean—Forest) initiative illustrates the social arrangement that sought to compensate for a labor market inefficiency. In 2013, ARAUCO established the first Training and Education Center for Forestry Workers in the Quirihue commune of Chile's Bío Bío region. This initiative includes training on the operation of forestry machinery. It results from an alliance between SENCE (the National Service for Training and Employment) and Emplea Foundation (which works under the Hogar de Cristo charity institution). The program design and construction result from the Labor Ministry, ARAUCO, and CORMA (Chilean Wood Corporation) collaboration. The company sought to satisfy the demand for an estimated 400 forestry professionals by the end of the decade (ARAUCO, 2013). The program's distinctiveness is that ARAUCO invites the Mapuche community members to receive a specific training program, and later they participate and consult for the company's forestry operations (ARAUCO, 2018).

The concurrent socioeconomic crises in the region alter labor markets in particular ways. During the downturns, workers' income suffers from severe damages, which implies a detriment in their social protection just as economic inequality increases in the region. The following two examples show how local companies take the lead and exert pressure in their organizational networks to ensure workers' income.

Antofagasta (Chilean—Mining) seeks to ensure quality employment. In January 2020, the company adopted the Ethical Minimum Wage policy for on-site contractors. It consists of paying their employees two-thirds above Chile's minimum wage. The company expects to benefit around 3,200 families, many of whom live near its operations. Antofagasta also requires contractors and subcontractors to provide their employees with health and life insurance and, in some cases, to support their children's education. Additionally, they must also comply with the UK's Modern Slavery Act or subject to risk sanctions or even lose the company's contract (Antofagasta Minerals, 2019).

Natura & Co. (Brazilian—Cosmetics) has the goal of providing to the consultants (salesforce) of its entire business group (The Body Shop, Avon, and Aesop) not just the minimum wage but a fair income. Natura & Co. measures Brazilian consultants' income by the living wage concept (the minimum amount necessary to live a dignified life). The Body Shop reported that it would be paying Real Living Wage rates to all UK stores staff. The Real Living Wage is 25% higher than the National Living Wage. Meanwhile, Aesop (a recent Australian acquisition) reports that it has concluded an assessment to establish a living wage standard in all the markets it operates in (Natura & Co., 2019).

The literature emphasizes the increasing partnerships between corporations and governments to contribute to the social and economic grand challenges (Davila, Rodriguez-Lluesma, & Elvira, 2018; Stahl et al., 2020). Additionally, given the limited governmental policies on income distribution, organizations require more attention to assure income stability and equality. However, the approach of SRHRM in Latin America is to promote collaboration among various societal actors to establish structures to improve labor market institutional effectiveness. Thus, SRHRM assures the protection of current and future workers rather than jobs.

The Stakeholder Perspective

The stakeholder perspective opens the scope of action—and responsibility—of the organization beyond the traditional input-output model (Donaldson & Preston, 1995). The main argument in this perspective is that organizations interact with various constituencies and connect with them through influence mechanisms. Then, research focuses on who the organizational stakeholders are and how organizations interact with them.

Freeman's well-known definition of a stakeholder is "A stakeholder in an organization is any group or individual who can affect or is affected by the achievement of the organization's objectives" (1984, p. 46). Primary organizational stakeholders are shareholders, suppliers, employees, and clients. Moreover, organizations always include governments and communities in general (Freeman, 1984). However, for organizations, stakeholders' saliency determines their importance and is composed of power, legitimacy, or urgency (Mitchell, Agle, & Wood, 1997). Research shows a hierarchical relationship between salient stakeholders and the organization, in which the organization plays the central role (Donaldson & Preston, 1995; Mitchell et al., 1997).

The stakeholder perspective supports the advancement of SRHRM in Latin America because it builds on the organization's moral responsibility within its context. Davila and Elvira (2012, 2018) constructed the Latin America HRM model based on this perspective. The main argument of the model is that HRM and the primary stakeholders acknowledge the needs and demands of multiple stakeholders, which also are the beneficiaries of the HRM policies and practices.

Davila and Elvira (2009) introduced the term "silent stakeholders" to refer to those individuals or groups that may lack resources to defend their interests and be unnoticed by business organizations. Such stakeholders refer to individuals of the socioeconomic sector or community with no legitimacy or power (Davila & Molina, 2017) but dependent on the employment relationship (Davila & Elvira, 2009, 2018). Thus, HRM impacts the community via employees. The community members are employees' families, children of school age, workers of other companies, and members of disadvantaged communities, among others (Davila & Elvira, 2012, 2018).

The underpinnings of the Latin American HRM model are: (a) investment in employees—salary and benefits levels as well as education, training, and development; (b) efforts to operate within a cooperative labor relations framework; and (c) CSR practices centered on the community (Davila & Elvira, 2012, 2018). One can observe that the model presents a precise alignment with the dimensions of human development as defined by the United Nations (UN): education, health, and living conditions. According to the United Nations Development Program (UNDP), human development is about enriching human life. The focus of action is on the people and their capabilities instead of the economy (UNDP, 2020a). The UNDP created the Human Development Index (HDI) to measure the countries' average achievement on human development's critical dimensions. The education dimension is measured using schooling years for adults aged 25 years and more and expected years of education for school-age children. The health dimension is assessed by life expectancy at birth. The gross national income per capita measures the standard of the living dimension (UNDP, 2020b). See Table 6.3 for how the Latin American countries' HDI score on average in the period 1990–2018.

Latin American companies' commitment to the region's human development is usually tied to the country's economic history, culture, and traditions (Logsdon, Thomas, & Van Buren III, 2006). Building on the stakeholder perspective, the region's economic history offers evidence of the role of SRHRM that provides for human development (Davila, Rodriguez-Lluesma, & Elvira, 2018). The history of the industrialization of Northern Mexico in the early 20th century portrays how companies invested and created institutions for human development following the path of employees, families, and community (Davila, Rodriguez-Lluesma, & Elvira, 2018).

Table 6.3 Latin American Countries: Human Development Index Scores Average (HDI) (1990–2018)

HDI Rank (2018)	Country	Last 28 years (Average)
48	Argentina	0.808
114	Bolivia	0.649
79	Brazil	0.721
42	Chile	0.806
79	Colombia	0.712
68	Costa Rica	0.755
85	Ecuador	0.722
124	El Salvador	0.640
126	Guatemala	0.588
132	Honduras	0.590
76	Mexico	0.742
126	Nicaragua	0.601
98	Paraguay	0.685
82	Peru	0.717
57	Uruguay	0.781
96	Venezuela	0.732
	OECD	0.878
	World	0.688

Source: Created by the author based on the Human Development Data (1990–2018), accessed June 4, 2020 through http://hdr.undp.org/en/data

A hegemonic group of businessmen managed large industrial ventures, such as steel, glass, chemicals, and a brewery surrounded by precarious working conditions. The familial management style motivated major employers to adopt a welfare approach with their workers, providing facilities, and suitable working conditions (Saragoza, 1988). The companies offered attractive benefits to their employees, such as free or subsidized housing, company schools, recreational facilities, and essential medical services. Later, the companies escalated the benefits to daycare centers and primary schools to the workers' children, free medical services, pharmacies, night schools for adults, libraries, sports, other recreational facilities, and credit unions. Companies opened vocational schools inside their facilities to train their workers in technical jobs. Then, the companies opened the schools to serve the community and to train future workers.

Although there was a difference in the material benefits offered to high-skilled workers, lower-skilled workers also received other health services benefits. Some historians condemned such practices arguing that they deepened labor inequalities in modern Mexico (e.g., Rojas Sandoval, 1997). Another argument against this welfare state in Mexico's early industrialization is that it was somehow intended for workers to stay in the country and thus avoid the diaspora to the United States of America in search of better living conditions (Saragoza, 1988).

However, Mexican businessmen installed cooperative labor relations, shortened the workday from 14 to 12 hours, and then to 10 hours. Such labor policies and practices were mainly attributed to the influence of the Papal Bull of 1891 (Rerum Novarum), which promoted harmony between labor and capital. Under this labor context, leading companies' employees rarely challenged their employers (Saragoza, 1988). Following the harmony principle between labor and capital, in 1918, the Cuauhtemoc brewery (today FEMSA) promoted a workers' cooperative for savings and investment. The cooperative granted diverse services to the workers and their families, including an employee savings plan matched by the company, scholarships, health services, health and life insurances, pension plans, sports tournaments, and a housing loan program (Salinas, 2018). In 1972, the housing program turned into the FEMSA's Workers' Housing Heritage (PAVITAC). From 1972 to 2004, it built more than 1,880 houses and awarded more than 8,000 credits for acquisition, improvements, and payment of houses' liabilities (FEMSA, 2005). In 2009, FEMSA ended the housing program and transferred its employees' accounts to the National Housing Fund for Workers Institute (INFONAVIT) (Salinas, 2018). The INFONAVIT is a state initiative funded through payroll taxes.

Gruma (Mexican—Tortilla Maker), in its Costa Rican operations, implemented the Zero Extreme Poverty program targeting employees that lived in conditions of extreme poverty. The program included technical and financial training, psychological care, a Child Care Network, scholarships, and housing bonds for more than 400 families, both the employees' company and the community (Gruma, 2014).

The evidence shown here uncovers three themes. First, there was a moral commitment from the early businessmen toward the employees, families, and community. Second, the welfare approach provides the workers with benefits to cover their basic needs, education, health, and living conditions such as housing. In other words, companies provide benefits along with the HDI dimensions. Third, labor initiatives prove to be the foundations of the current social contract of contextual stakeholders' welfare expectations. Thus, under the stakeholder perspective, SRHRM's role is that of the provider for human development.

Final Remarks

This chapter presents evidence that suggests that the two main research lines of SRHRM limit the concept's potential to improve Latin American development via HRM. One of the research lines seeks that HRM practices influence employees to develop socially responsible behaviors and attitudes to support the organization's CSR objectives. The other research line seeks that employees achieve personal fulfillment and satisfaction through their jobs. However, both research lines continue addressing how an employee-centered CSR approach can benefit the organization with limited understanding of the employee human development or societal advancement. Thus, this chapter expands the SRHRM concept and analyzes the employees' context and the CSR employee-centered practices of several Latin American firms. The analysis of the employees' context included data from the human capital (skills and health), institutional voids (market inefficiencies), and stakeholder perspective (salient and silent stakeholders). In each contextual view, there is an SRHRM role that performs best under every circumstance.

One can observe that SRHRM is quite active in various spheres of Latin American society. Although many of the SRHRM activities could be attributed to the organization's CSR strategy, the difference is that SRHRM is employee-context-centered. Moreover, under the three disciplinary views analyzed here, SRHRM could establish the CSR agenda in this region.

This chapter informs HR practitioners how to redefine their HRM systems role supported by a broader CSR view. At the same time, it informs CSR how to approach an employee context-based social responsibility activity. Moreover, SRHRM advises strategic HRM on how to develop the appropriate social infrastructure for human capital. SRHRM compensates for the institutional voids of the Latin American economies' recent openings promoting the mechanisms that make labor markets more effective. The chapter then traces the history of the paternalistic social contract's underpinnings that SRHRM provides for the workers, families, and community human development.

Although the three perspectives depart from different theoretical positions, and data indicates a particular gap in the employees' development as individuals, the three views seem to complement each other. For example, when seeking to fulfill the lack of appropriate labor skills, we found companies that build schools, others organize a network of institutions to provide the right training or install a program of scholarships. Still, later the companies expanded such initiatives to benefit the employees' family members and the community. The same pattern of CSR activities applies to health services or living standards. Thus, the three perspectives might explain similar CSR actions. However, the activities' meaning might differentiate one viewpoint over the other and expand in different ways the SRHRM concept.

Finally, for a company that wants to develop the social responsibility capability in Latin America, the advice is to act according to the context. First, create the social infrastructure for human capital development, compensate for labor markets voids, provide local stakeholders' needs and demands, and lastly focus on employees' attitudes and behaviors toward organizational CSR.

References

Antofagasta Minerals. 2019. *2019 sustainability report.* Retrieved December 27, 2020, from www.antofagasta.co.uk/sustainability/sustainability-report-library/

ARAUCO. 2013. *2013 sustainability report.* Retrieved August 2, 2020, from www.arauco.cl/_file/file_3420_15176-report-arauco-ingles-2013.pdf

ARAUCO. 2018. *2018 sustainability report.* Retrieved August 2, 2020, from www.arauco.cl/wp-content/uploads/2017/07/REPORTE_SUSTENTABILIDAD_2018_INGLES.pdf

Becker, G. S. 2009. *Human capital: A theoretical and empirical analysis, with special reference to education.* Chicago, IL. University of Chicago Press.

Berliner, D., Greenleaf, A., Lake, M., & Noveck, J. 2015. Building capacity, building rights? State capacity and labor rights in developing countries. *World Development,* 72: 127–139.

Bondy, K., & Starkey, K. 2014. The dilemmas of internationalization: Corporate social responsibility in the multinational corporation, *British Journal of Management,* 25(1): 4–22.

Castellacci, F. 2015. Institutional voids or organizational resilience? Business groups, innovation, and market development in Latin America. *World Development,* 70: 43–58.

CEPAL. 2020.*Sectores y empresas frente al COVID-19: Emergencia y reactivación* [Sectors and companies facing COVID-19: Emergency and reactivation].Retrieved December 26, 2020, from https://repositorio.cepal.org/bitstream/handle/11362/45734/4/S2000438_es.pdf

Contreras, M. E. (Ed.). 2004. *Corporate social responsibility in the promotion of social development experiences in Asia and Latin America.* Washington, DC: Inter-American Development Bank. Retrieved March 30, 2016, from https://publications.iadb.org/handle/11319/206

Davila, A. 2019. Analysis of the MNEs' social practices in Latin America: Implications for development studies research. In P. Lund-Thomsen, M. W. Hansen, & A. Lindgreen (Eds.), *Business and development studies: Issues and perspectives* (pp. 310–328). London: Routledge.

Davila, A., & Elvira, M. M. 2012. Latin American HRM model. In C. Brewster & W. Mayrhofer (Eds.), *Handbook of research in comparative human resource management* (pp. 478–493). Cheltenham, UK: Edward Elgar Publishing.

Davila, A., & Elvira, M. M. 2018. Revisiting the Latin American HRM model. In C. Brewster, W. Mayrhofer, & E. Farndale (Eds.), *Handbook of research in comparative human resource management* (2nd ed., pp. 393–407). Cheltenham, UK: Edward Elgar Publishing.

Davila, A. & Molina, C. 2017. From silent to salient stakeholders: A study of a coffee cooperative and the dynamic of social relationships. *Business & Society*, 56(8): 1195–1224.

Davila, A., Rodriguez-Lluesma, C., & Elvira, M. M. 2018. Engaging stakeholders in emerging economies: The case of Multilatinas. *Journal of Business Ethics,* 152(4): 949–964.

Donaldson, T., & Preston, L. E. 1995. The stakeholder theory of the corporation: Concepts, evidence, and implications. *Academy of Management Review*, 20(1): 85–91.

FEMSA. 2005. *Primer informe de responsabilidad social* [First social responsibility report]. Retrieved September 26, 2016, from www.femsa.com/sites/default/files/IS_2005.pdf

Flores, L. 2015. Ternium formará cientos de técnicos en Pesquería [Ternium will train hundreds of technicians in Pesqueria.] *El economista*. Retrieved Mayo 15, 2020, from www.eleconomista.com.mx/estados/Ternium-formara-cientos-de-tecnicos-en-Pesqueria-20150722-0188.html

Freeman, R. E. 1984. *Strategic management: A stakeholder approach.* Boston, MA: Pitman.

Gifford, B., & Kestler, A. 2008. Toward a theory of local legitimacy by MNEs in developing nations: Newmont mining and health sustainable development in Peru. *Journal of International Management,* 14(4): 340–352.

González, A. 2020. Arranca Ternium su hospital Covid-19 [Ternium starts its Covid-19 hospital.] *El norte*. Retrieved April 18, 2020, from www.elnorte.com/arranca-ternium-su-hospital-covid-19/ar1922355

Granovetter, M. 2005. Business groups and social organization. In N. Smelser & R. Swedberg (Eds.), *Handbook of economic sociology* (2nd ed., pp. 429–450). Princeton, NJ: Russell Sage Foundation and Princeton University Press.

Gruma. 2014. *Informe annual* [Annual report]. Retrieved July 25, 2016, from www.gruma.com/media/610277/ia_gruma_2014_espa_ol.pdf

Jamali, D., & Karam, C. 2018. Corporate social responsibility in developing countries as an emerging field of study, *International Journal of Management Reviews,* 20(1): 32–61.

Khanna, T., & Palepu, K. G. 1997. Why focused strategies may be wrong for emerging markets. *Harvard Business Review,* 75(4): 41–51.

Khanna, T., & Palepu, K. G. 2010. *Winning in emerging markets: A road map for strategy and execution.* Boston, MA: Harvard Business Press.

Khanna, T., & Rivkin, J. 2001. Estimating the performance effects of business groups in emerging markets. *Strategic Management Journal,* 22(1): 45–74.

Lawler, E. E. 2009. Make human capital a source of competitive advantage. *Organizational Dynamics,* 38(1): 1–7.

Logsdon, J. M., Thomas, D. E., & Van Buren III, H. J. 2006. Corporate social responsibility in large Mexican firms. *Journal of Corporate Citizenship*, 21: 51–60.

Mexichen. 2009. *2009 Sustainable development report.* Retrieved August 2, 2020, from www.orbia.com/4a0e09/siteassets/6.-sustainability/sustainability-reports/2009/desarrollosustentable2009_ing.pdf

Mitchell, R. K., Agle, B. R., & Wood, D. J. 1997. Toward a theory of stakeholder identification and salience: Defining the principle of who and what really counts. *Academy of Management Review,* 22(4): 853–886.

Natura & Co. 2019. *2019 report Natura & Co.* Retrieved December 27, 2020, from https://ri.naturaeco.com/en/publications-and-documents/reports/

Nyberg, A. J., & Wright, P. M. 2015.50 years of human capital research: Assessing what we know, exploring where we go. *Academy of Management Perspectives,* 29(3): 287–295.

Orlitzky, M., & Swanson, D. L. 2006. Socially responsible human resource management. Charting new territory. In J. R. Deckop (Ed.), *Human resource management ethics* (pp. 3–25). Charlotte, NC: Information Age.

Phillips, S., Mehrez, G., & Moissinac, V. 2006. *Mexico: Selected issues.* **Country report.** Washington, DC: International Monetary Fund. Retrieved May 1, 2007, from www.imf.org/external/pubs/ft/scr/2006/cr06351.pdf

Rojas Sandoval, J. 1997. *Fábricas pioneras de la industria en Nuevo León* [Pioneer factories in the state of Nuevo Leon]. Monterrey, Mexico: UANL Press.

Salinas, C. 2018. *Cien años de sociedad (1918–2018).* [One hundred years of a cooperative (1918–2018)]. Centro de Información Empresarial de Nuevo León. Retrieved December 29, 2020, from https://centrocien.wordpress.com/2018/03/23/cien-anos-de-sociedad/

Saragoza, A. M. 1988. *The Monterrey elite and the Mexican state, 1880–1940.* Austin, TX: University of Texas Press.

Shen, J. 2011. Developing the concept of socially responsible international human resource management. *International Journal of Human Resource Management,* 22(06): 1351–1363.

Stahl, G. K., Brewster, C. J., Collings, D. G., & Hajro, A. 2020. Enhancing the role of human resource management in corporate sustainability and social responsibility: A multi-stakeholder, multidimensional approach to HRM. *Human Resource Management Review,* 30(3): 100708.

Ternium. 2020. *La escuela técnica Roberto Rocca en México* [The technical school Roberto Rocca in Mexico]. Retrieved Mayo 2, 2020, from https://mx.ternium.com/es/sustentabilidad/comunidad/educacion/

UNDP. 2020a. *What is human development? About human development.* Retrieved April 20, 2020, from http://hdr.undp.org/en/humandev

UNDP. 2020b. *Human development index (HDI).* Retrieved April 20, 2020, from http://hdr.undp.org/en/content/human-development-index-hdi

Wang, S. L., & Cuervo-Cazurra, A. 2017. Overcoming human capital voids in underdeveloped countries. *Global Strategy Journal,* 7(1): 36–57.

7 A Stakeholder Approach to Strategic Human Resource Management in Latin America

Michel Hermans and Julián Darío Díaz Avendaño

Introduction

Organizations around the world have embraced the idea of investing in their employees through High Performance Work Practices (HPWPs) to enact worker attitudes and behaviors toward enhanced performance outcomes (Dastmalchian et al., 2020) and Latin American firms are not an exception (De la Garza-Cardenas, Zeron-Felix, & Sanchez-Tovar, 2018; de Miranda Castro et al., 2020; Raineri, 2017). Although researchers have identified some variation in the individual practices that are considered HPWPs, they generally include careful employee selection, intensive training, development-oriented feedback, performance-based pay, and worker involvement in decision-making (Langevin-Heavey et al., 2013; Posthuma, Campion, Masimova, & Campion, 2013). Implementation of these practices is associated with increased knowledge, skills, and abilities (KSAs), and empowers and motivates workers. These effects are reflected in intermediate outcomes such as employee commitment, job satisfaction or turnover, as well as more distant firm performance outcomes (Jiang, Lepak, Hu, & Baer, 2012) and—to some extent—in employee well-being (Guerci, Hauff, & Gilardi, 2019).

Notwithstanding the growth of HPWPs implementation in Latin America, insights regarding the factors that drive the implementation of HPWPs, and their effects in organizations obtained from studies conducted in other regions need to be contextualized (Hermans, 2018). Latin America's common Ibero-Catholic cultural background and its history of macro-economic volatility and pronounced swings in the political arena have led scholars to propose a "Latin American management model" (Elvira & Davila, 2005). The idea of a common work culture with traits such as an emphasis on social relationships and respect for authority, proved to be fertile ground for cross-cultural HRM research across the region. However, over time the assumption of a monolithic regional culture has become increasingly inadequate. Migration within, from and into the region, increased recognition of historically less visible or vocal groups, shifts in religious beliefs, steepening differences in the region's income distribution, and stratified access to education and technology are drivers of growing cultural heterogeneity. Moreover, multinationals from less traditional countries of origin for the region—such as China, Malaysia, Turkey, or Russia—have brought their human resource management practices (Beamond, Farndale, & Härtel, 2020). Finally, a growing group of Latin American firms has internationalized its operations (Aguilera, Ciravegna, Cuervo-Cazurra, & Gonzalez-Perez, 2017), which has implications for their HRM strategies. Consequently, researchers have repeatedly called for using alternative theoretical lenses to analyze the factors that shape decisions regarding the implementation of HRM practices, including transaction cost economics, comparative institutional theory, and pragmatic humanism (Davila & Elvira, 2012; Hermans, 2018).

More recently, scholars have highlighted the importance of stakeholders to understanding management in Latin America (e.g., (Arora & De, 2020; Davila, Rodriguez-Lluesma, & Elvira, 2018). A stakeholder approach to management suggests that individuals or groups can affect or are affected by the pursuit and achievement of an organization's goals (Freeman, 1984). Stakeholder theory challenges neo-classical economics definitions of value as consumer or producer surpluses and, instead, focuses on the exchange of resources to consider both value creation and value appropriation (Garcia-Castro & Aguilera, 2015). Because of its focus on identifiable actors and resource exchanges, stakeholder theory complements other theories of organization (Ulrich & Barney, 1984). In particular, it connects well with the resource based view (Barney, 1991); the predominant theoretical underpinning of SHRM research.

In this chapter, we argue that an understanding of SHRM in Latin America requires consideration of stakeholders, who are not only internal to the organization, such as managers and employees, but also of external stakeholders, such as investors, governments, and clients. We consider that organizations interact with these stakeholders within the broader context of the political economy of the countries in which they operate. Accounting for industry-related effects and firm-level strategies, we posit that the extent to which organizations consider stakeholders' interests will be associated with investments in employees through HPWPs. We analyze data obtained from 1,643 respondents of a survey that was administered across 14 Latin American countries.

SHRM in Latin America: Looking Outside the "Black Box"

Ever since scholars recognized the importance of HRM practices to firms' ability to execute business strategies, they have pointed to the importance of understanding the conditioning effects of organizational and contextual characteristics on the use of and outcomes obtained from HRM practices (Schuler & Jackson, 1987; Wright & McMahan, 1992). However, following difficulties to find compelling evidence for contextual or strategic fit of HRM practices (Gerhart, 2007), many SHRM scholars focused their efforts on "unpacking the black box," pursuing an understanding of the intra-organizational mechanisms through which HPWPs have effects on employee and organizational outcomes (Jiang, Takeuchi, & Lepak, 2013; Peccei & Van De Voorde, 2019).

The intra-organizational focus is problematic for the development of an understanding of SHRM in Latin America because the contextual dynamics of the region and approaches to management of firms that operate in it differ from those of other regions (Aguinis et al., 2020; Hermans & Borda Reyes, 2020). As the field initially developed in the US, basic assumptions regarding decision-making in firms and interaction between firms and other actors in the business context were implicitly imprinted on SHRM research (Brewster, 2007). For example, firms in the US historically faced low state intervention, low union membership, developed capital markets, or corporate governance that separates ownership from management of firms. These characteristics may not apply to firms that operate in other countries, especially in emerging markets such as Latin America.

To overcome this limitation, researchers increasingly attempt to bridge SHRM research with comparative HRM research (Batt & Hermans, 2012). Focusing on the contextual determinants of variation in firms' implementation of HRM practices, researchers draw on comparative institutional approaches (Amable, 2003; Hall & Soskice, 2001; Whitley, 1999). Such approaches suggest that firms are embedded in a social context in which "formal and informal rules, regulations, norms, and understandings . . . constrain and enable behavior" (Morgan, Campbell, Crouch, Pedersen, & Whitley, 2010, p. 2). While the Latin American institutional landscape is less charted as compared to other regions (Morgan, 2011), important advances have been made. Researchers emphasize how shifts in labor legislation, institutional voids, and firm strategies shape labor market institutions (e.g., (Castellacci, 2015; Posner, Patroni, & Mayer, 2018), while weak links between worker skill development, labor supply, and wages (Fernández & Messina, 2018) further inform the context for human resource management.

In-depth analysis of specific institutions has allowed for understanding their association with HRM outcomes but inform to a lesser extent on the interaction between institutions and how they affect decision-making at the level of the individual firm (Hermans, 2018). Toward that end, more comprehensive frameworks (e.g., (Fainshmidt, Judge, Aguilera, & Smith, 2018; Schneider, 2009; Schneider & Karcher, 2010) focus on the characteristics of and interactions between actors in the political economy. For example, Schneider (2009) suggests that institutional actors in the Latin American political economy respond to a hierarchical logic that is dictated by the elites that own national or regional business groups. Fainshmidt et al. (2018) not only highlight the role of owner-families in the political economy of many Latin American countries but also identify countries in which the state occupies a central role—such as Argentina and arguably Venezuela—and market-based coordination in Chile. The central role of different identifiable actors to the structuring of the Latin American political economy and the "rules of the game" that condition the interaction between the actors has consequences for firm strategies and, hence, for SHRM. Consequently, we suggest that theoretical frameworks that account for the influence of these salient actors can improve our understanding of SHRM in the region.

Stakeholder Theory and SHRM

Stakeholder theory (e.g., Donaldson & Preston, 1995; Freeman, 1984) proposes that organizations interact with "groups and individuals who can affect or are affected by the achievement of the firm's objectives" (Freeman, 1984, p. 25). A stakeholder approach conceptualizes the firm as a nexus of multilateral contracts over time (Freeman & Evan, 1990), which implies that the firm obtains access to resources through exchanges with known organizational stakeholders. Stakeholder theory posits that firms that take into account and accommodate stakeholder interests will have better access to required resources, and will obtain competitive advantage (Donaldson & Preston, 1995). Moreover, a firm's set of sound ongoing relationships with stakeholders is considered a valuable and socially complex resource in itself, which contributes to and sustains a firm's competitive advantage (Hillman & Keim, 2001).

Internal Stakeholders' Influence on SHRM

Consideration of stakeholder interests is not new to the SHRM literature (e.g., Beer, Spector, Lawrence, Mills, & Walton, 1984; Colakoglu, Lepak, & Hong, 2006; Hermans, Wright, Ulrich, & Sioli, 2009). Investment in workers by implementing HPWPs reflects the importance of human capital to an organization, as well as its commitment to the employment relationship (Huselid, 1995; Tsui, Pearce, Porter, & Tripoli, 1997). Employees are expected to reciprocate such investments by developing knowledge, skills, and abilities that organization needs, displaying commitment and organizational citizenship behaviors, and participating in decision-making and problem solving toward value creation. This exchange allows for value creation within the organization. Employees' human capital underlies organizational capabilities and allows for competitive advantage when such human capital is firm-specific, causally ambiguous and socially complex (Wright, Dunford, & Snell, 2001). However, more recently researchers have identified conditions under which firm-specific human capital may not lead to competitive advantage, or when generic human capital may (Campbell, Coff, & Kryscynski, 2012). This requires organizational decision makers to assess not only how exchanges with employees can create value but also who appropriates such value before they make investments in the employment relationship (Coff, 1997, 1999).

In the case of firms that operate in Latin America, consideration of how investment in employees and their managers may enhance their exchanges with the organization is important because several contextual characteristics affect both value creation and appropriation. Labor markets are characterized by a high degree of regulation but poor enforcement, low skill levels, high turnover, weak unions, and high levels of informality (Ronconi, 2012; Schneider & Karcher, 2010). Focusing more specifically on segments within labor markets, we distinguish between informal and formal work, and low versus high knowledge requirements to understand how consideration of managers and workers' interests may relate to HPWPs implementation. Informal sector work is prevalent in Latin America, with some countries reporting participation rates in excess of 60% (ECLAC, 2019). Companies that operate in the formal sector often rely on informal sector suppliers and distributors to create a more flexible organizational system that can react to the pronounced changes in the economic cycle that characterize the region (Schneider & Karcher, 2010). In the absence of formal employment contracts, investments in employees will be limited and focused on meeting short-term operational needs. On the job training and variable compensation based on meeting performance goals and avoiding turnover when the economy is strong are replaced by assigning less or no work during economic downturns.

Employment in Latin America's formal sector is characterized by a longer-term orientation, which increases the likelihood for HPWPs to yield positive outcomes. HRM practices in the public sector and in sectors where unions represent workers, such as mining, oil, and gas or food processing tend to be focused on working conditions, compensation, and worker representation. However, employers in more knowledge intensive sectors, such as financial services, the emerging IT cluster, or high added-value manufacturing, and individual firms that aim to un-commoditize to achieve international competitiveness (Cuervo-Cazurra et al., 2019) have a stronger incentive to invest in workers. The desirability of employment at these firms, which are often multinationals, is higher (Newburry, Gardberg, &

Sanchez, 2014), enabling these firms to recruit more selectively. Employers in knowledge intensive sectors are also more informed about global best practices regarding developmental feedback and variable pay within the context of performance management (Mellahi, Frynas, & Collings, 2016). However, Latin American knowledge workers increasingly switch employers or transition to working independently, which may withhold employers from investing in the development of transferrable generic human capital. Finally, growing international exposure of firms that operate in the region is not necessarily associated with positive employee outcomes. Emerging market multinationals are more likely to complement their existing management team with foreign executives (Arp, 2014) and may discourage their employees' aspirations for internal career development (Alvarado-Vargas, Hermans, & Newburry, 2020).

Whether due to un-commoditization strategies, international competition or increased automation of basic jobs, the exchanges between firms that operate in Latin America and their employees have become more important. Taken together, we suggest the following:

Hypothesis 1: Firms in Latin America that pay more attention to internal stakeholders are more likely to implement HPWPs.

External Stakeholders' Influence on SHRM

One of the premises of strategic HRM is that an organization plans its human resources deployments and activities to enable the organization to achieve its goals (Wright & McMahan, 1992). Examinations of the relationships between strategies and SHRM in the context of market entry strategies (Han, Kang, Oh, Kehoe, & Lepak, 2018) or changing production strategies (Youndt, Snell, Dean, & Lepak, 1996) suggest that organizations can use HRM practices to develop the capabilities that allow for implementing their strategy. By investing in the workers, who perform the organizational processes that underlie capabilities, they enhance the skills people individually and collectively possess, and the behaviors people engage in (Wright et al., 2001).

The development of organizational capabilities is an evolutionary and dynamic process (Helfat & Peteraf, 2009). In contexts characterized by high volatility, such as Latin America, organizations need to constantly adjust and reconfigure their asset structure, and to accomplish the necessary "internal and external transformation ahead of competition" (Teece, Pisano, & Shuen, 1997, p. 520). The organizational capacity to purposefully create or modify the firm's resource base, or dynamic capabilities (Eisenhardt & Martin, 2000), is generally considered from an intra-organizational perspective.

However, researchers increasingly acknowledge that, in addition to managerial decisions, actors who are external to the organization influence the reconfiguration process as well. Organizations interact with clients, suppliers, governments, and investors to obtain information that allows for effective bundling of resources into capabilities. Additionally, interaction with external stakeholders allows for access to required resources, such as raw materials, capital, or market access. Within these interactions, stakeholders exert influence on how the organization uses resources and develops organizational capabilities (Coff, 1999) and claim a share of the rents to be generated (Coff, 2010). We expect organizations that pay more attention to external stakeholders as a means to reconfigure capabilities to also invest more in HPWPs to develop the human capital resources that allow for implementing such adjustments.

Researchers of the political economy of Latin America typically highlight the importance of interactions between firms and stakeholders in capital markets, in product markets, labor markets, and regulators (e.g., Fainshmidt et al., 2018; Schneider, 2009; Schneider & Karcher, 2010). A recent study on Latin American business groups suggests that financial performance results from active approaches to managing both internal and external stakeholders in the region's complex economic and institutional context (Rodriguez & Torres, 2020). Focusing more specifically on labor relations and HRM, scholars point to the importance of specific actors in the region's political economy in firm-level decision-making regarding investments in employees (Carnes, 2014; Davila & Elvira, 2015; Hermans, 2018; Ronconi, 2012).

A first type of actor refers to governments at both the national, regional, and local levels of society. Scholars associate the marked heterogeneity in organizational outcomes in the region with public policies and governments' ability to develop institutional and economic frameworks that allow for controlling inflation, collecting taxes, and providing access to credit and other public forms of support (Bianchi, Mingo, & Fernandez, 2018). Moreover, governments administer large and highly visible organizations, such as Pemex in Mexico, Entel in Bolivia, CODELCO in Chile, or Ecopetrol in Colombia (Musacchio, Ayerbe, & García, 2015), and are shareholders of private firms through publicly administered pension funds or development agencies such as BNDES in Brazil or CORFO in Chile. Consideration of regulation and direct involvement of governments in firm-level decision-making reflect a longer-term and contextually embedded strategic orientation. This characteristic generally applies to larger organizations but, in Latin America, government policies and programs also play important roles in supporting internationalization strategies of small and medium-sized enterprises that need to develop specific capabilities (Cardoza, Fornes, Farber, Gonzalez Duarte, & Ruiz Gutierrez, 2016; Finchelstein, 2017). We expect firms' consideration of governments and regulators in decision-making regarding HRM to be positively associated with investments in employees through HPWPs.

Second, access to capital markets in Latin America conditions firm decision-making significantly. Scholars have pointed to the role of the state as a preferred source of capital when compared to private sources (Lazzarini et al., 2015). Likewise, Latin American business groups frequently owned banks that allowed for internal funding (Del Angel, 2016), or accessed foreign capital markets (Schmukler, Gozzi, & De la Torre, 2007). As different providers of capital have divergent interests, firms in Latin America that need to secure access to capital for future investments will signal consideration of such interests in their decision-making processes. We expect that, within a general context of securing access to capital for investments in the development and reconfiguration of capabilities, firms are more likely to invest in employees through HPWPs as well.

Third, while horizontal diversification strategies continue to be widespread characteristics of firms in Latin America, the corporate landscape has changed significantly since the 1990s. A growing group of firms has achieved competitiveness pursuing vertical integration strategies, entering global value chains, or developing networked forms of operation (Brenes, Ciravegna, & Pichardo, 2018). These organizational strategies require close coordination with suppliers and distributors and involve restructuring of resources. While this process has been found to be slow (McDermott & Corredoira, 2010), those firms that do seek upgrading based on "learning by supplying" strategies (Alcacer & Oxley, 2014) will pay more attention to their value chain partners. Within this upgrading, we expect firms to invest in employees through HPWPs.

Fourth, firms in Latin America have historically focused on clients in domestic markets, with the exception of exports of bulk commodities. Import substitution policies allowed local firms and subsidiaries of MNCs to delay technological upgrading and diversification of their product and services offerings. The pro-market reforms of the 1990s and the commodities bonanza of the following decade enhanced offerings, although higher quality products were often imported and aimed at more affluent clients. More recently, the number of firms in Latin America that compete in international markets has increased (Aguilera et al., 2017). This involved a need to develop capabilities that allow for responding to the needs of more sophisticated clients and changing preferences. Investments in more client-responsive capabilities likely involve investments in employees through HPWPs as well.

In sum, we argue that in a volatile context such as Latin America, firms frequently need to reconfigure their capabilities to remain competitive. This process involves consideration of external stakeholders as a means to obtain information regarding the business environment and access to resources. Investments in HPWPs allow for the development of a workforce that has the necessary KSAOs to effectively implement changes. Hence, we expect that:

> *Hypothesis 2: Firms that pay more attention to their external stakeholders will be more likely to invest in their employees through HPWPs.*

Method

Sample

While the economies of Latin America comprise a wide variety of employment arrangements, we chose to focus on formal employers distributed across different industries. Data for our study were obtained in the context of a global online survey of HR professionals and line managers conducted in 2016. In order to avoid single-rater bias we required individual-level responses from at least four HR professionals and four line managers of each participating organization. Consequently, the sample is biased toward organizations that are considered large in the Latin American context. The final sample consisted of 1,643 individual raters, subdivided between 878 HR professionals, and 765 line managers. Raters were employed at 82 organizations distributed across manufacturing, services and other industries such as agriculture, mining, or energy.

Measures

High-Performance Work Practices Implementation

We followed guidelines suggested by Langevin-Heavey et al. (2013) to measure the implementation of HPWPs. We derived items from the commitment HRM practices scale as developed by Lepak & Snell (2002) as it includes the most common human resource management practices such as selection, training, incentive compensation, employee involvement, or empowerment, and participative work design. Also, Posthuma et al.'s (2013) cross-cultural ranking of most frequently used items in measures of HPWPs overlap to a large extent with the practices included in this scale. Thus, we asked line managers to rate their agreement with statements that referred to the implementation of HPWPs in the organization they worked for. The specific items are listed in the Appendix and the scale's internal consistency (Cronbach's alpha) was 0.71. Finally, ratings of individual line managers were clustered within business units. The ICC(1) value was 0.29, the ICC(2) value was 0.80, and the F-test was significant (Bliese, 2000). Hence, we analyzed our data accounting for such clustering.

Internal Stakeholder Consideration

We measured the extent to which organizations considered internal stake-holder interests in the design and implementation of HRM practices by asking at least four professionals in the HR department: "To what extent does your HR department consider and involve the following stakeholders in the design and delivery of HRM practices?" Ratings were obtained for (1) employees and (2) line managers on a scale that ranged from 1 (= very little extent) to 5 (very large extent). The scale's internal consistency was 0.81. Given that we aggregated ratings of individual HR raters into a unit-level variable we report the aggregation statistics. The ICC(1) value was 0.18 and the ICC(2) value was 0.68. Additionally, the F-test was significant, justifying aggregation.

External Stakeholder Consideration

Similarly, we measured the extent to which organizations considered external stakeholder interests in the design and implementation of HRM practices by asking at least four professionals in the HR department: "To what extent does your HR department consider and involve the following stakeholders in the design and delivery of HRM practices?" Ratings were obtained for (1) governments and regulators, (2) investors or owners, (3) organizations in the value chain (e.g., suppliers or distributors), and (4) clients. The scale's internal consistency was 0.79. This variable was also based on aggregated ratings of individual HR respondents. ICC(1) and ICC(2) values were 0.12 and 0.58, respectively. As the F-test was significant as well, aggregation was justified.

Control Variables

Acknowledging the importance of institutional variation within the Latin American region, we controlled for sub-types of institutional contexts following the classification proposed by Fainshmidt et al. (2018). Likewise, we controlled for different types of activity using a broad sub-grouping of organizations into manufacturing, services, and extractive industries. Finally, organizations that compete based on efficiency are likely to invest less in their employees. We included a control variable to account for this effect.

Results

We report the descriptive statistics and correlations between the variables of our study in Table 7.1. For tests of our hypotheses, we relied on hierarchical multi-level modelling (Raudenbush & Bryk, 2002). We invoked the MIXED procedure in SPSS 26.0 because of its versatility for the analysis of hierarchical linear models for continuous outcome variables and because it allows for an easy inclusion of crossed fixed coefficients.

We report the results of our hypotheses tests below, in Table 7.2. First, we suggested that organizations in Latin America that give more consideration to their internal stakeholders will be more likely to implement HPWPs. A comparison of model 2, in which we test the effects of our control variables, with model 3, in which we include internal stakeholder consideration, shows a positive and significant effect ($\beta = 1.29$; $p < .01$). This finding provides support for our first hypothesis. Second, we tested whether consideration given to Latin American organizations' external stakeholders was associated with HPWPs implementation. The results of model 4 indicate that, even when controlling for the effect of internal stakeholder consideration, there is a positive and significant association between external stakeholder consideration and HPWPs implementation ($\beta = 0.53$; $p < .01$). Hence, our second hypothesis was supported as well.

Given the importance of contextual factors to the analysis of SHRM in an international context, we report findings regarding the control variables as well. We did not find support for effects on HPWPs implementation for any comparative institutional sub-type. Even in the case of model 2, which only includes the control variables, different types of organization of the political economy of Latin American countries were not associated with the implementation of HPWPs. A similar finding was obtained for our broad classification of industries. The results did not provide evidence for higher levels of HPWPs implementation for any type of activity. By contrast, firm-level strategies that emphasize operational efficiency were associated with lower levels of investment in employees through HPWPs ($\beta_{Model\ 2} = -1.35$; $p < .01$; $\beta_{Model\ 4} = -0.85$; $p < .10$).

While model 2, which included only the control variables, suggested that firm-level strategies were more important to explanations of HPWPs implementation than contextual characteristics, we conducted additional analyses to test whether context influenced the extent to which the organizations in our sample considered specific stakeholders. To this end, we conducted MANOVA analyses in which we explored differences in consideration

Table 7.1 Descriptive Statistics and Bi-Variate Correlations

	Mean	SD	1	2	3	4	5	6	7	8	9
1. Emergent LME	0.03	0.06									
2. State Led	0.41	0.47	-0.07								
3. Family Led	0.57	0.46	-0.05	-0.99*							
4. Extractive Industries	0.27	0.45	-0.08	0.04	-0.03						
5. Manufacturing	0.21	0.41	0.33*	0.13	-0.17	-0.31*					
6. Services	0.52	0.50	-0.19	-0.14	0.17	-0.64*	-0.54*				
7. Efficiency-oriented Strategy	0.16	0.25	-0.12	0.15	-0.13	0.36*	-0.17	-0.19			
8. Internal Stakeholder Consideration	8.15	1.40	0.07	-0.10	0.09	0.02	-0.02	0.00	0.02		
9. External Stakeholder Consideration	17.03	2.89	-0.01	0.08	-0.08	0.08	0.11	-0.16	-0.16	0.48*	
10. HPWPs Implementation	25.60	4.98	0.01	-0.19	0.19	0.03	-0.05	0.02	0.01	0.30*	0.38*

$N = 82$

* Correlation is significant at the 0.05 level
* Correlation is significant at the 0.01 level

Table 7.2 Results of Crossed Fixed Effects Analysis of HPWP Implementation

	Model 1			Model 2			Model 3			Model 4		
	β	se		β	se		β	se		β	se	
Intercept	25.60	0.42	**	25.67	1.34	**	15.27	1.43	**	6.06	3.00	**
Institutional context												
Family-led Economies				0.15	1.15		−0.29	1.07		0.31	1.13	
State-led Economies				0.07	1.20		−0.25	1.09		0.24	1.14	
Emergent Liberal Market Economy				—			—			—		
Industries												
Services				0.28	0.99		0.14	0.72		0.01	0.64	
Manufacturing				−0.05	1.18		0.09	0.82		−0.01	0.66	
Extractive Industries and Agriculture				—			—			—		
Efficiency-oriented strategy				−1.35	0.52	**	−1.12	0.47	*	−0.85	0.48	†
Stakeholder consideration												
Internal Stakeholder Consideration							1.29	0.10	**	1.23	0.29	**
External Stakeholder Consideration										0.53	0.16	**
−2 Restricted Log Likelihood	4,694.58			4,680.13			4,654.65			4,645.71		
Akaike's Information Criterion	4,698.58			4,684.13			4,658.65			4,649.71		

** $p < 0.01$
* $p < 0.05$
† $p < 0.10$
$n = 765$, within 82 business units

given to individual and grouped stakeholder types. Bootstrapped results (1,000 iterations) did not indicate any significant differences or post-hoc contrast between comparative institutional sub-types for our grouped stakeholder measures (internal versus external). The same analysis at the level of ungrouped items did not suggest any differences either. By contrast, a MANOVA that examined differences across industries at the level of individual stakeholder-oriented items suggested that consideration of customers and partners in the value chain such as suppliers and distributors was higher in manufacturing sectors. In service sectors, governmental regulators were given more consideration.

Stakeholder Consideration in SHRM in Latin America

Organizations relate to their context through exchanges with identifiable and often visible actors. Stakeholder theory (Freeman, 1984) suggests that the importance of such exchanges has consequences to how decisions are made within an organization. Within a sample of 1,643 respondents, we found support for a stakeholder approach in the context of strategic HRM in Latin America. Organizations that consider the interests of internal stakeholders, such as employees and their managers, are more likely to make investments in employees by implementing HPWPs. Additionally, and controlling for internal stakeholders, we found that consideration of external stakeholders, such as clients, investors or owners, government agencies, suppliers, and distributors, is associated with higher levels of HPWPs implementation as well.

Investments in employees and the HRM practices used to manage them suggest that exchanges with workers are important to the achievement of an organization's goals. Consideration of these internal stakeholders as a potential source of competitive advantage has been—and continues to be—a characteristic of the SHRM field (Kaufman, 2015). In that sense, our first finding is largely a confirmation of an underlying assumption of the SHRM field in the context of Latin America. However, the association between external stakeholder consideration and investment in HPWPs suggests that organizations in Latin America seek to align the development of human capital resources with stakeholder interests. In highly volatile contexts, such as Latin America, organizations need to frequently reassess how they create value for their exchange partners. For example, at a given moment clients may value efficiency, innovation, or service. HPWPs can contribute to the development of more efficient operations (Kehoe & Wright, 2013), enhance creativity (Dong, Yaping, Jing, & Jia-Chi, 2017) and an organizational climate for service (Chuang & Liao, 2010). Consequently, investing in workers through HPWPs may not only contribute to the development of the specific KSAOs required to operate the processes that underly organizational capabilities (Wright et al., 2001) but also allow for changing such capabilities when the organization's strategy shifts.

Although the conditions for management research are improving (Aguinis et al., 2020), SHRM research in Latin America is scarce when compared to the body of research focused on the US, Europe, or even to other emerging markets in Asia or Eastern Europe (Posthuma et al., 2013). We identify two difficulties that need to be addressed for further progress. First, the underexplored institutional context of Latin America, the frequent changes that occur in it and some firms' ability to avoid, bend or shape the "rules of the game," make it difficult to determine the role of context in SHRM research (Hermans, 2018). Our results suggest that firm-level strategies focused on operational efficiencies are more strongly associated with differences in HPWPs implementation than country-level or industry-related institutions. We acknowledge that our sample comprised mainly organizations that are considered large within the Latin American context and, arguably, progressive in their approach to HRM. This may have biased our findings toward firm-level managerial discretion, which may not apply to smaller organizations.

Second, SHRM research is generally focused on intermediate, employee-oriented outcomes that can be related to enhanced market competitiveness or financial results. However, firms that operate in Latin America do not necessarily share such definitions of value creation (Hermans & Borda Reyes, 2020). The role of families as owner-managers in Latin American firms (see: Aguilera et al., 2017) may warrant consideration of factors such as family identity, social status, or maintaining the ability to exert political influence. Also, organizations that are managed by families are more likely to forego short-term performance to preserve the firm as a source of income for heirs (Poletti-Hughes & Williams, 2019). A stakeholder approach to SHRM challenges common approaches to measuring performance as it requires researchers to account for the wide range of possible reasons of owners and managers to invest in HPWPs. Qualitative or mixed method approaches to SHRM research may provide insight on this.

Our study contributes to a broader stream of research of internationally oriented HRM research that aims to understand how workers can be managed effectively in different contexts (e.g., Collings, Mellahi, & Cascio, 2018; Hermans, 2018; Sidani & Al Ariss, 2014; Thite, Budhwar, & Wilkinson, 2014). Given the importance of highly visible actors, including families of owner-managers and governments, to the political economies of Latin America (Fainshmidt et al., 2018; Schneider & Karcher, 2010) and a renewed interest in stakeholder management approaches in strategy research

(Garcia-Castro & Aguilera, 2015), we explored the association between consideration of stakeholders and HPWPs implementation in this region. Within a sample of 1,643 respondents we find support for consideration of both internal and external stakeholders as factors that are related to HPWPs implementation. This finding not only suggests that firms in Latin America aim to enhance performance by investing in human capital resources, but they also make such investments in response to strategic interactions with external stakeholders, including clients, investors, governments, and suppliers and distributors.

As volatility in global markets requires firms across the globe to reconfigure organizational capabilities effectively, we encourage researchers of SHRM—both in emerging and more developed markets—to look beyond organizational boundaries. Renewed interest in vertical fit (Han et al., 2018) and the notion of HR ecosystems (Snell & Morris, 2018) suggest a need to focus on visible actors in the business environment and link their interests to strategies for human capital resources management.

References

Aguilera, R. V., Ciravegna, L., Cuervo-Cazurra, A., & Gonzalez-Perez, M. A. 2017. Multilatinas and the internationalization of Latin American firms. *Journal of World Business*, 52(4): 447–460.

Aguinis, H., Villamor, I., Lazzari, S. G., Vassolo, R. S., Amorós, J. E., & Allen, D. G. 2020. Conducting management research in Latin America: Why and what's in it for you? *Journal of Management*, 46(5): 615–636. doi: 10.1177/0149206320901581.

Alcacer, J., & Oxley, J. 2014. Learning by supplying. *Strategic Management Journal*, 35(2): 204.

Alvarado-Vargas, M. A., Hermans, M., & Newburry, W. 2020. What's in it for me? Perceived career opportunities resulting from firm internationalization. *Journal of Business Research,* 117: 201–211.

Amable, B. 2003. *The diversity of modern capitalism.* Oxford: Oxford University Press.

Arora, P., & De, P. 2020. Environmental sustainability practices and exports: The interplay of strategy and institutions in Latin America. *Journal of World Business*, 55(4): 101094.

Arp, F. 2014. Emerging giants, aspiring multinationals, and foreign executives: Leapfrogging, capability building, and competing with developed country multinationals. *Human Resource Management*, 53(6): 851–876.

Barney, J. 1991. Firm resources and sustained competitive advantage. *Journal of Management*, 17(1): 99–120.

Batt, R., & Hermans, M. 2012. Global human resource management: Bridging strategic and institutional perspectives. In J. J. Martocchio, A. Joshi, & H. Liao (Eds.), *Research in personnel and human resource management* (Vol. 31, pp. 1–52). Bingley, UK: Emerald Publishing.

Beamond, M. T., Farndale, E., & Härtel, C. E. J. 2020. Frames and actors: Translating talent management strategy to Latin America. *Management and Organization Review*, 16(2): 405–442.

Beer, M., Spector, B., Lawrence, P. R., Mills, D. Q., & Walton, R. E. 1984. *A conceptual view of HRM. Managing human assets*. New York: Free Press.

Bianchi, C., Mingo, S., & Fernandez, V. 2018, October. Strategic management in Latin America: Challenges in a changing world. *Journal of Business Research*, 105: 306–309.

Bliese, P. D. 2000. Within-group agreement, non-independence, and reliability: Implications for data aggregation and analysis. In K. J. Klein & S. W. J. Kozlowski (Eds.), *Multilevel theory, research, and methods in organizations* (pp. 349–381). San Francisco, CA: Jossey-Bass.

Brenes, E. R., Ciravegna, L., & Pichardo, C. A. 2018, March. Managing institutional voids: A configurational approach to understanding high performance antecedents. *Journal of Business Research*, 105, 345–358.

Brewster, C. 2007. Comparative HRM: European views and perspectives. *The International Journal of Human Resource Management*, 18(5): 769–787.

Campbell, B. A., Coff, R., & Kryscynski, D. 2012. Rethinking sustained competitive advantage from human capital. *Academy of Management Review*, 37(3): 376–395.

Cardoza, G., Fornes, G., Farber, V., Gonzalez Duarte, R., & Ruiz Gutierrez, J. 2016. Barriers and public policies affecting the international expansion of Latin American SMEs: Evidence from Brazil, Colombia, and Peru. *Journal of Business Research*, 69(6): 2030–2039.

Carnes, M. E. 2014. *Continuity despite change: The politics of labor regulation in Latin America* (1st ed.): Stanford, CA: Stanford University Press.

Castellacci, F. 2015. Institutional Voids or Organizational Resilience? Business Groups, Innovation, and Market Development in Latin America. *World Development*, 70: 43–58.

Chuang, C.-H., & Liao, H. 2010. Strategic human resource management in service context: Taking care of business by taking care of employees and customers. *Personnel Psychology*, 63(1): 153–196.

Coff, R. W. 1997. Human assets and management dilemmas: Coping with hazards on the road to resource-based theory. *The Academy of Management Review*, 22(2): 374.

Coff, R. W. 1999. When competitive advantage doesn't lead to performance: The resource-based view and stakeholder bargaining power. *Organization Science*, 10(2): 119–133.

Coff, R. W. 2010. The coevolution of rent appropriation and capability development. *Strategic Management Journal*, 31: 711–733.

Colakoglu, S., Lepak, D., & Hong, Y. 2006. Measuring HRM effectiveness: Considering multiple stakeholders in a global context. *Human Resource Management Review*, 16(2): 209–218.

Collings, D. G., Mellahi, K., & Cascio, W. F. 2018. Global talent management and performance in multinational enterprises: A multilevel perspective. *Journal of Management*, 45(2): 540–566.

Cuervo-Cazurra, A., Carneiro, J., Finchelstein, D., Duran, P., Gonzalez-Perez, M. A., Montoya, M., . . . Newburry, W. 2019. Uncommoditizing strategies by emerging market firms. *Multinational Business Review*, 27(2): 141–177.

Dastmalchian, A., Bacon, N., McNeil, N., Steinke, C., Blyton, P., Satish Kumar, M., . . . Varnali, R. 2020. High-performance work systems and organizational performance across societal cultures. *Journal of International Business Studies*, 51(3): 353–388.

Davila, A., & Elvira, M. M. 2012. Latin American HRM models. In C. Brewster & W. Mayrhofer (Eds.), *Handbook of research on comparative human resource management*. Cheltenham, UK: Edward Elgar Publishing.

Davila, A., & Elvira, M. M. 2015. Human resource management in a kinship society: The case of Latin America. In F. Horwitz & P. Budhwar (Eds.), *Handbook of Human Resource management in emerging markets*. Cheltenham, UK: Edward Elgar Publishing.

Davila, A., Rodriguez-Lluesma, C., & Elvira, M. M. 2018. Engaging Stakeholders in Emerging Economies: The Case of Multilatinas. *Journal of Business Ethics*, 152(4): 949–964.

De la Garza-Cardenas, M. H., Zeron-Felix, M., & Sanchez-Tovar, Y. 2018. El impacto de la gestión del recurso humano en la competitividad de la pyme en el noreste de México. *Revista Perspectiva Empresarial*, 5(2): 27–36.

de Miranda Castro, M. V., Lopes de Araujo, M., Miguens Ribeiro, A., Demo, G., & Murce Meneses, P. P. 2020. Implementation of strategic human resource management practices: A review of the national scientific production and new research paths. *REGE Revista de Gestão*, 27(3): 229–246.

Del Angel, G. A. 2016. The nexus between business groups and banks: Mexico, 1932–1982. *Business History*, 58(1): 111–128.

Donaldson, T., & Preston, L. E. 1995. The stakeholder theory of the corporation: Concepts, evidence, and implications. *Academy of Management Review*, 20: 65–91.

Economic Commission for Latin America and the Caribbean (ECLAC) and International Labour Organization (ILO). 2019. The future of work in Latin America and the Caribbean: Old and new forms of employment and challenges for labour regulation. *Employment Situation in Latin America and the Caribbean*, 20.

Eisenhardt, K. M., & Martin, J. A. 2000. Dynamic capabilities: What are they? *Strategic Management Journal*, 21(10–11): 1105–1121.

Elvira, M. M., & Davila, A. 2005. Emergent directions for human resource management research in Latin America. *International Journal of Human Resource Management*, 16(12): 2265–2282.

Fainshmidt, S., Judge, W. Q., Aguilera, R. V., & Smith, A. 2018. Varieties of institutional systems: A contextual taxonomy of understudied countries. *Journal of World Business*, 53(3): 307–322.

Fernández, M., & Messina, J. 2018. Skill premium, labor supply, and changes in the structure of wages in Latin America. *Journal of Development Economics*, 135: 555–573.

Finchelstein, D. 2017. The role of the State in the internationalization of Latin American firms. *Journal of World Business*, 52(4): 578–590.

Freeman, R. E. 1984. *Strategic management: A stakeholder approach*. Boston, MA: Pitman.

Freeman, R. E., & Evan, W. M. 1990. Corporate governance: A stakeholder interpretation. *Journal of Behavioral Economics*, 19: 337–359.

Garcia-Castro, R., & Aguilera, R. V. 2015. Incremental value creation and appropriation in a world with multiple stakeholders. *Strategic Management Journal*, 36(1): 137–147.

Gerhart, B. 2007. Horizontal and vertical fit in human resource systems. In C. Ostroff & T. A. Judge (Eds.), *Perspectives on organizational fit* (pp. 317–348). New York: Psychology Press.

Guerci, M., Hauff, S., & Gilardi, S. 2019. High performance work practices and their associations with health, happiness and relational well-being: Are there any tradeoffs? *The International Journal of Human Resource Management*, 1–31.

Hall, P. A., & Soskice, D. 2001. *Varieties of capitalism: The institutional foundations of comparative advantage*. Oxford: Oxford University Press.

Han, J. H., Kang, S., Oh, I.-S., Kehoe, R., & Lepak, D. 2018. The goldilocks effect of strategic human resource management? Optimizing the benefits of a high-performance work system through the dual alignment of vertical and horizontal fit. *Academy of Management Journal*, 62.

Helfat, C., & Peteraf, M. 2009. Understanding dynamic capabilities: Progress along a developmental path. *Strategic Organization*, 7(1): 91–102.

Hermans, M. 2018. Comparative HRM research in South America: A call for comparative institutional approaches In C. Brewster, W. Mayrhofer, & E. Farndale (Eds.), *Handbook of research on comparative human resource management* (2nd ed., pp. 427–444). Cheltenham, UK: Edward Elgar Publishing.

Hermans, M., & Borda Reyes, A. 2020. A value creation perspective on international business in Latin America: Directions for differentiation between emerging market multinationals. *Multinational Business Review*, 28(2): 157–175.

Hermans, M., Wright, P. M., Ulrich, D., & Sioli, A. L. 2009. Enhancing HRM practices: A stakeholder approach. *Proceedings of Academy of Management, USA*, 1–6. https://doi.org/10.5465/ambpp.2009.44256587

Hillman, A. J., & Keim, G. D. 2001. Shareholder value, stakeholder management, and social issues: What's the bottom line. *Strategic Management Journal*, 22(2): 125–140.

Huselid, M. A. 1995. The impact of human resource management practices on turnover, productivity, and corporate financial performance. *The Academy of Management Journal*, 38(3): 635–672.

Jiang, K., Lepak, D. P., Hu, J. I. A., & Baer, J. C. 2012. How does human resource management influence organizational outcomes? A meta-analytic investigation of mediating mechanisms. *Academy of Management Journal*, 55(6): 1264–1294.

Jiang, K., Takeuchi, R., & Lepak, D. P. 2013. Where do we go from here? New perspectives on the Black box in strategic human resource management research. *Journal of Management Studies*, 50(8): 1448–1480.

Kaufman, B. E. 2015. Evolution of strategic HRM as seen through two founding books: A 30th anniversary perspective on development of the field. *Human Resource Management*, 54(3): 389–407.

Kehoe, R., & Wright, P. M. 2013. The impact of high-performance human resource practices on employees' attitudes and behaviors. *Journal of Management*, 39(2): 366–391.

Langevin-Heavey, A., Beijer, S. E., Federman, J., Hermans, M., Klein, F., McClean, E., & Martinson, B. 2013. Measurement of human resource practices: Issues regarding scale, scope, source and substantive content. In J. Paauwe, D. E. Guest & P. M. Wright (Eds.), *HRM and performance: Achievements & challenges*. Chichester, West Sussex, UK: John Wiley & Sons.

Lazzarini, S. G., Musacchio, A., Bandeira-de-Mello, R., & Marcon, R. 2015. What do state-owned development banks do? Evidence from Brazil, 2002–2009. *World Development*, 66: 237–253.

Lepak, D. P., & Snell, S. A. 2002. Examining the human resource architecture: The relationships among human capital, employment, and human resource configurations. *Journal of Management*, 28(4): 517–543.

Lui, D., Gong, Y., Zhou, J., & Huang, J. 2017. Human resource systems, employee creativity, and firm innovation: The moderating role of firm ownership. *Academy of Management Journal*, 60(3): 1164–1188. https://doi.org/10.5465/amj.2015.0230

McDermott, G. A., & Corredoira, R. A. 2010. Network composition, collaborative ties, and upgrading in emerging-market firms: Lessons from the Argentine autoparts sector. *Journal of International Business Studies*, 41(2): 308–329.

Mellahi, K., Frynas, J. G., & Collings, D. G. 2016. Performance management practices within emerging market multinational enterprises: The case of Brazilian multinationals. *The International Journal of Human Resource Management*, 27(8): 876–905.

Morgan, G. 2011. Comparative capitalisms: A framework for the analysis of emerging and developing economies. *International Studies of Management & Organization*, 41(1): 12–34.

Morgan, G., Campbell, J., Crouch, C., Pedersen, O. K., & Whitley, R. 2010. *The Oxford handbook of comparative institutional analysis*. Oxford: Oxford University Press.

Musacchio, A., Ayerbe, E. I., & García, G. 2015. *State-owned enterprise reform in Latin America issues and possible solutions*. IDB Discussion Paper 401. Washington, DC: Inter-American Development Bank.

Newburry, W., Gardberg, N. A., & Sanchez, J. I. 2014. Employer attractiveness in Latin America: The association among foreignness, internationalization and talent recruitment. *Journal of International Management*, 20(3): 327–344.

Peccei, R., & Van De Voorde, K. 2019. The application of the multilevel paradigm in human resource management—outcomes research: Taking stock and going forward. *Journal of Management*, 45(2): 786–818.

Poletti-Hughes, J., & Williams, J. 2019. The effect of family control on value and risk-taking in Mexico: A socioemotional wealth approach. *International Review of Financial Analysis*, 63: 369–381.

Posner, P. W., Patroni, V., & Mayer, J.-F. 2018. *Labor politics in Latin America: Democracy and worker organization in the neoliberal era.* Gainesville: University of Florida Press.

Posthuma, R. A., Campion, M. C., Masimova, M., & Campion, M. A. 2013. A high performance work practices taxonomy: Integrating the literature and directing future research. *Journal of Management*, 39(5): 1184–1220.

Raineri, A. 2017. Linking human resources practices with performance: The simultaneous mediation of collective affective commitment and human capital. *International Journal of Human Resource Management*, 28(22): 3149–3178.

Raudenbush, S. W., & Bryk, A. S. 2002. *Hierarchical linear models: Applications and data analysis methods.* Thousand Oaks, CA: Sage Publications.

Rodriguez, C., & Torres, J. 2020, July. Central coordination and profitability in large Latin American business groups. *Journal of Business Research*, 1–11.

Ronconi, L. 2012. Globalization, domestic institutions, and enforcement of labor Law: Evidence from Latin America. *Industrial Relations*, 51(1): 89–105.

Schmukler, S. L., Gozzi, J. C., & De la Torre, A. 2007. *Capital market development: Whither Latin America?* Washington, DC: The World Bank.

Schneider, B. R. 2009. Hierarchical market economies and varieties of capitalism in Latin America. *Journal of Latin American Studies*, 41(3): 553–575.

Schneider, B. R., & Karcher, S. 2010. Complementarities and continuities in the political economy of labour markets in Latin America. *Socio-Economic Review*, 8(4): 623–651.

Schuler, R. S., & Jackson, S. E. 1987. Linking competitive strategies with human resource management practices. *Academy of Management Executive*, 1(3): 207–219.

Sidani, Y., & Al Ariss, A. 2014. Institutional and corporate drivers of global talent management: Evidence from the Arab Gulf region. *Journal of World Business*, 49(2): 215–224.

Snell, S., & Morris, S. 2018. Time for realignment: The Hr ecosystem. *Academy of Management Perspectives*.

Teece, D. J., Pisano, G., & Shuen, A. 1997. Dynamic capabilities and strategic management. *Strategic Management Journal*, 18(7): 509–533.

Thite, M., Budhwar, P., & Wilkinson, A. 2014. Global HR roles and factors influencing their development: Evidence from emerging Indian IT services multinationals. *Human Resource Management*, 53(6): 921–946.

Tsui, A. S., Pearce, J. L., Porter, L. W., & Tripoli, A. M. 1997. Alternative approaches to the employee-organization relationship: Does investment in employees pay off? *Academy of Management Journal*, 40(5): 1089–1121.

Ulrich, D., & Barney, J. B. 1984. Perspectives in organizations: Resource dependence, efficiency, and population. *Academy of Management Review*, 9: 471–481.

Whitley, R. 1999. *Divergent capitalisms: The social structuring and change of business systems*: Oxford, UK: Oxford University Press.

Wright, P. M., Dunford, B. B., & Snell, S. A. 2001. Human resources and the resource based view of the firm. *Journal of Management*, 27(6): 701–721.

Wright, P. M., & McMahan, G. C. 1992. Theoretical perspectives for strategic human resource management. *Journal of Management*, 18(2): 295–320.

Youndt, M. A., Snell, S. A., Dean, J. W., & Lepak, D. P. 1996. Human resource management, manufacturing strategy, and firm performance. *The Academy of Management Journal*, 39(4): 836–866.

Index

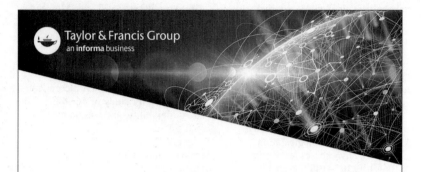